PUCCINI
and His Operas

PUCCINI
and His Operas

EDITED BY STANLEY SADIE

MACMILLAN REFERENCE LIMITED, LONDON
ST. MARTIN'S PRESS, INC, NEW YORK, NY

Published in Great Britain by
MACMILLAN REFERENCE LTD
25 Eccleston Place, London, SW1W 9NF

Basingstoke and Oxford
Companies and representatives throughout the world

British Library Cataloguing in Publication Data
Puccini and his operas - (Composers and their operas)
1. Puccini, Giacomo, 1858—1924. 2. Operas. 3. Composers - Italy - Biography
I. Sadie, Stanley, 1930—
782.1´092
ISBN 0-333-790227

Published in the United States and Canada by
ST. MARTIN'S PRESS, INC
175 Fifth Avenue, New York, NY 10010

ISBN 0-312-244185

A catalog record for this book is available from the Library of Congress

Typesetting by The Florence Group, Stoodleigh, Devon, UK

Printed and bound in Britain by Cambridge University Press, Cambridge.

CONTENTS

PREFACE

This volume is one of a series drawn from *The New Grove Dictionary of Opera* (1992). That dictionary, in four volumes, includes articles on all significant composers of opera and on their individual operas (as well as many other topics). We felt that it would serve the use of a wider readership to make this material available in a format more convenient for the lover of opera and also at a price that would make it accessible to a much larger number of readers.

The most loved, and most performed, of opera composers are (in chronological order) Mozart, Verdi, Wagner and Puccini, who form the central topics of these volumes. The volumes each include chapters on the composer's life (with particular emphasis on his operatic activities) and a chapter on each of his operas. In some cases, the availability of additional space has made it possible for us to include, additionally, information that provides a fuller context for the composer and his work. Not for Verdi, who (perhaps unfortunately) composed so many operas that space did not permit any additions. And in the case of Wagner, whose operas demand quite extensive discussion, it was possible to add material only on his original singers and of course on Bayreuth.

For the Mozart volume, however, in which only a relatively modest number of operas call for extensive treatment, we were able to include material on virtually all his singers (excluding only those on whom we are almost totally ignorant) and on his interesting array of librettists, as well as some background on cities in which his music was heard. And for Puccini, there is material not only on librettists and singers but also on the most important composers among his Italian contemporaries, men whose music is still in the repertory (for instance the composers of *Cavalleria rusticana* and *Pagliacci*).

The authors of the chapters in these books are leading authorities on their subjects. The Mozart volume is chiefly the work of Julian Rushton, the Verdi of Roger Parker and the Wagner of Barry Millington, while the Puccini principal author is Julian Budden. Writers of the shorter sections are individually acknowledged within the book. We are grateful to all of them for permitting the re-use of their work.

STANLEY SADIE
London, 1999

ILLUSTRATIONS

Plate 1 – Giacomo Puccini (right), with (left to right) Giulio Gatti-Casazza, David Belasco and Arturo Toscanini in New York aat the time of the première of *La fanciulla del West* in December 1910

Plate 2 – Page from the disposizione scenica (production book) for the original production of Puccini's *Manon Lescaut* at the Teatro Regio, Turin, 1 February 1893: the setting for Act 3 (Le Havre, a square near the harbour) [Biblioteca Braidense (photo Giancarlo Costa)]

Plate 3 – Poster for the first production of Puccini's *Madama Butterfly* by L. Metlicovitz [Giancarlo Costa]

Plate 4 – *Suor Angelica*: final scene of the original production (designed by Pietro Stroppa) at the Metropolitan opera, New York, 14 December 1918, with Geraldine Farrar as Sister Angelica [Metropolitan Opera Archives]

Plate 5 – Claudia Muzio in the title role of Puccini's *Tosca* [Stuart-Liff Collection]

Plate 6 – Enrico Caruso as Canio in Leoncavallo's *Pagliacci* [Stuart-Liff Collection]

Plate 7 – *La bohème* (Puccini), Act 3 (the Barrière d'Enfer), in the original production at the Teatro Regio, Turin, 1 February 1896: from *L'illustrazione italiana* (23 February 1896) [Biblioteca Braidense (photo Giancarlo Costa)]

Plate 8 – Autograph score of a page from Cavaradossi's aria, 'Recondita armonia', from Act 1 of Puccini's *Tosca* (1900) [Ricordi Historical Archive]

CONTRIBUTORS

A.L.	Andrew Lamb
B.R.	Barbara Reynolds
C.S.	Christopher Smith
J.B.	Julian Budden
J.Bl.	John Black
J.M.	Jürgen Maehder
M.G.	Michele Girardi
M.S.	Matteo Sansone
R.M.	Richard Macnutt
R.P.	Roger Parker

CHRONOLOGY OF PUCCINI'S LIFE AND OPERAS

1858

22 December   Born in Lucca into a family of musicians

1874   Enters Istituto Musicale Pacini

1877   Composes *Plaudite populi* (motet for baritone, mixed chorus and orchestra)

1880   Enters Milan Conservatory and studies composition with Antonio Bazzini

1883   Composes *Capriccio sinfonico*

1884

31 May   Première of *Le villi*, Milan, Teatro dal Verme

26 December   Second version of *Le villi*, Turin, Regio

Sets up house with Elvira Geminiani, wife of a Luccan grocer

1889   Visits Bayreuth with the conductor Franco Faccio to advise on cuts for La Scala production of *Die Meistersinger*

21 April   *Edgar*, Milan, Scala; second version 1892, Ferrara, Comunale, 28 February; third (definitive) version 1905, Buenos Aires, Opera, 8 July

1893

1 February   *Manon Lescaut*, Turin, Regio

1896

1 February   *La bohème*, Turin, Regio

1900

14 January   *Tosca*, Rome, Costanzi

1903   Marries Elvira Geminiani on the death of her husband

1904

17 February   *Madama Butterfly*, Milan, Scala; second version, Brescia, Grande, 28 May; third version 1905, London, Covent Garden, 10 July; fourth version 1906, Paris, Opéra Comique (Feydeau), 28 December

1910

10 December   *La fanciulla del West*, New York, Metropolitan

1917

27 March   *La rondine*, Monte Carlo, Opéra

1918

14 December   *Il trittico*: *Il tabarro*, *Suor Angelia*, *Gianni Schicchi*, New York, Metropolitan

1924

29 November   Puccini dies in Brussels, while undergoing surgery for throat cancer, leaving *Turandot* unfinished

1926

25 April   *Turandot*, Milan, Scala

Biography

Giacomo Puccini

Giacomo Antonio Domenico Michele Secondo Maria Puccini was born at Lucca on 22 December 1858 into a family that had supplied his native city with cathedral organists and composers for four generations. He was taught the rudiments of music by his maternal uncle, Fortunato Magi, his father having died when he was five years old. He sang as a treble in the choir of the Cathedral of San Martino and the church of San Michele; at 14 he was able to deputize for organists in the neighbourhood. At the Istituto Musicale Pacini, which he entered in 1874, he studied under Carlo Angeloni, Magi's successor as director, a respectable composer mainly of motets and masses.

Lucca's cultural life was remarkably rich for a provincial town. Operatic fare was supplied at its three theatres at different times of the year. No less important for Puccini's future was a strong tradition of spoken drama, with regular visits by Italy's most distinguished touring companies, offering a repertory that reached from Vittorio Alfieri and Carlo Goldoni to the latest Parisian products of the Dumas *père et fils*, Sardou and Alfred de Musset. At a time when the canons of play and opera were drawing ever closer together, their influence on the future composer of *La bohème* and *Tosca* can hardly be overestimated; indeed it was to his early familiarity with a wide range of dramatic literature that Puccini later owed his flair for discovering the operatic possibilities of plays that he saw performed in a language of which he understood not a word.

Luccan opera, by contrast, was for the most part poorly mounted and inadequately sung by second-rate artists, often recruited locally. It was not until he saw a performance of Verdi's *Aida* in Pisa in 1876 that Puccini awoke to the full possibilities of the genre and decided once and for all where his future lay. That same year saw his first composition of any significance: a prelude in E minor for orchestra, the autograph of which is in the private collection of Natale Gallini, Milan. In 1877 he wrote the motet for baritone, mixed chorus and orchestra *Plaudite populi*, which was performed at a students' concert in April that year. The motet was repeated the following year, with a newly-

3

composed Credo that was subsequently incorporated in the *Messa a quattro voci* of 1880, Puccini's passing-out piece for the Istituto Musicale Pacini. Known for a long time only to Puccini scholars, this work was first published in 1951 under the title *Messa di gloria*. Though not especially devotional in character, it shows a sureness of musical touch and a complete control of material. The Kyrie and Agnus Dei were recycled in *Edgar* and *Manon Lescaut* respectively.

With the aid of a grant from the Queen of Italy, augmented by a subsidy from a bachelor relation, Puccini proceeded to the Milan Conservatory, although he was well over the age limit for entrance (he was in his 22nd year). He did well enough at the examination to be accepted into the senior composition class. His first teacher was the well-known violinist and composer Antonio Bazzini, one of the few Italian professors with a European background. For him Puccini composed a string quartet in Mendelssohnian style, only one movement of which survives. When in 1882 Bazzini succeeded to the directorship Puccini passed under the tuition of Amilcare Ponchielli, who, in the short time remaining to him (he died in 1886), did all he could to further Puccini's career in opera. However, the two principal fruits of his studies were a *Preludio sinfonico* in A major (1882) and the *Capriccio sinfonico* with which he graduated in 1883. Both show a new richness of orchestral imagination and a number of harmonic and melodic features that are characteristic of the mature composer. Of the *Capriccio*, which later provided the opening theme for *La bohème*, Milan's leading critic, Filippo Filippi, wrote in *La perseveranza* that it denoted a 'specifically symphonic talent'. Nonetheless, opera remained Puccini's goal.

THE FIRST OPERAS: 'LE VILLI', 'EDGAR' AND 'MANON LESCAUT'

That same year – 1883 – Puccini entered a competition for a one-act stage piece promoted by the publisher Edoardo Sonzogno. Ponchielli found him a librettist in the young 'scapigliato' poet Ferdinando Fontana, who took the subject from a short story, *Les willis*, by the French writer Alphonse Karr. Puccini declared himself delighted with it 'since it will mean working a good deal in the symphonic-descriptive vein, and that will suit me very well'. But despite Ponchielli's presence among the adjudicators the prize was awarded elsewhere and *Le villi* did not even receive an honourable mention. Fortunately friends and acquaintances subscribed to a performance in May 1884 at the Teatro Dal Verme, Milan, which prompted one critic to declare that 'Puccini could be the composer for whom Italy has been waiting a long time'. Filippi was again complimentary, adding, however, that 'Puccini's nature is essentially that of a symphonist and . . . he exaggerates the *symphonic element*, and frequently overloads the pedestal to the detriment of the statue'. Verdi wrote to a friend, Count Arrivabene, that he

had heard many good things said about the composer Puccini. It seems however that the symphonic element predominates in him. No harm in that! But here we should tread carefully. Opera is opera and symphony is symphony; and I don't think that in an opera it's a good idea to write a symphonic piece merely for the pleasure of making the orchestra dance.

The publisher Giulio Ricordi, however, was in no doubt that in the composer of *Le villi* he had found Verdi's successor. He persuaded Fontana and Puccini to expand it into two acts, in which form it achieved a modest circulation over the next few years. He also commissioned a new, full-length opera from poet and composer and arranged for the firm to provide Puccini with a monthly stipend so that he could compose the music at leisure. Until his death in 1912 Giulio Ricordi acted as the composer's 'guide, philosopher and friend', advising him on subjects, finding him librettists and smoothing out his perennial difficulties with them.

Puccini's letters home shed a revealing light on his enthusiasms at the time, *Carmen* ('a most beautiful opera') and *Dejanice*, by his fellow Luccan Alfredo Catalani ('the public don't go into ecstasies over it, but I say that artistically speaking it's a fine opera, and if they do it again I shall go back to see it'). Other formative influences noted by Ponchielli (without approval) were Massenet, evident in the soft suppleness of his vocal lines, and Wagner, for whom Puccini nurtured a lifelong admiration. In 1889 he accompanied the conductor Faccio to Bayreuth to advise on cuts for the forthcoming production at La Scala of *Die Meistersinger* (as *I maestri cantori di Norimberga*).

For their next collaboration Fontana and Puccini turned to a dramatic poem by Alfred de Musset, which became the four-act opera *Edgar*. Progress on the composition was painfully slow, largely due to domestic circumstances. Shortly after his mother's death in 1884 Puccini set up house with Elvira Geminiani, wife of a Luccan grocer, who brought with her two children. A year later their own son Tonio was born; but it was not until Geminiani's death in 1903 that the union was regularized. Eventually produced at La Scala in 1889, *Edgar* achieved a mere *succès d'estime*. The critics noted an advance on *Le villi*, especially in orchestral and harmonic resource, but admitted that in general the work was a disappointment. Puccini later condensed the four acts into three without, however, improving its fortunes. Ricordi was now under pressure from shareholders to withdraw Puccini's allowance; but he held firm, to find his faith in his protégé triumphantly vindicated by the immediate success of *Manon Lescaut* (1893, Turin). The opera's genesis had been more than usually tormented. Four librettists, including Ruggero Leoncavallo, had been successively involved in the text; and though the final product was effectively the work of Domenico Oliva and Luigi Illica it was decided to publish the libretto without an attribution. But the critics and public were unanimous in their praise. When the opera reached London in 1894 Bernard Shaw noted in *The World* that in it 'the domain of Italian opera is enlarged by an annexation of German territory', adding that 'Puccini looks to me more like the heir of Verdi than any of his rivals'. From that time Puccini's financial problems were at an end. He was able not only to repay Ricordi's advances in full but also to acquire a spacious villa at Torre del Lago, which was to remain his home for most of his life and has since become the composer's museum.

1894–1904: 'LA BOHÈME', 'TOSCA' AND 'MADAMA BUTTERFLY'

Unlike most of his contemporaries Puccini produced his operas at long intervals, partly because of his fastidiousness in choosing subjects, several of which he took up only to abandon after several months, and partly because of his constant demands for modification of the texts. Much of his time, too, was spent in hunting in the marshes round his new home and in trips abroad to supervise revivals of his works. For his librettos over the next decade Ricordi secured him the team of Luigi Illica, who worked out the scheme and drafted the dialogue, and the poet and playwright Giuseppe Giacosa, who put the lines into verse. The first fruit of their partnership was *La bohème* (1896, Turin), drawn from Henry Murger's picaresque novel of life among the artists of the Latin Quarter in Paris. The critics were cool, several of them finding in the opera's comparative restraint a certain falling-off of invention after the emotional ardour of *Manon Lescaut*. But the public soon took it to their hearts; and it quickly outstripped its predecessor in popularity abroad. Only in Vienna was it excluded for some years from the repertory, because of the hostility of Mahler, who much preferred Leoncavallo's treatment of the same subject.

Even before he had completed *La bohème* Puccini had already decided on an operatic setting of Victorien Sardou's play, *La Tosca*, for which Illica had in the meantime prepared a libretto for Alberto Franchetti. But although it had won the approval of Verdi Franchetti was dissatisfied with it and was persuaded without difficulty to hand it over to his rival. Over the next three years Illica and Giacosa shaped it to Puccini's requirements, and the opera was launched at the Teatro Costanzi, Rome, in 1900. Again the critics were guarded in their appraisal, but *Tosca* was soon going the rounds as successfully as *La bohème*. Here Puccini harnessed to his lyrical gift a leitmotif technique, loosely indebted to Wagner, in the service of a powerful, swiftly moving action, while transforming Sardou's mildly ridiculous heroine, conceived as a vehicle for the virtuosity of Sarah Bernhardt, into a credible and moving personality. Nor would it be the last time that Puccini succeeded in vastly improving on his literary source. For his next opera he turned to David Belasco's one-act play *Madame Butterfly* after seeing it performed in London. With the help of Illica and Giacosa he expanded the slender plot to the dimensions of a full evening's entertainment. Completion was delayed, however, by a severe motor accident, from which Puccini's slow recovery was found to be due to a diabetic condition that remained with him to the end of his life. When the première of *Madama Butterfly* eventually took place (1904, Milan), the opera was subjected to what Puccini described as 'a veritable lynching'. That the audience's hostility was deliberately engineered none of his biographers has ever doubted, though they are not prepared to say by whom. All the evidence points, however, to Ricordi's chief rival, Sonzogno, as the prime mover. Such members of the 'giovane scuola' as had flocked to his banner – Pietro Mascagni, Ruggero Leoncavallo, Umberto Giordano, Francesco Cilea – had by now clearly given their best work. None had equalled Ricordi's protégé in achieving three major successes in a row; a fourth was bound to be unwelcome. The few modifications that Puccini brought to the score for its second performance at Brescia that year would not have been sufficient to turn the tide in its favour, had the public's initial reaction to it been spontaneous. As it was, *Madama Butterfly* quickly joined its two predecessors as one of the cornerstones of the contemporary operatic repertory. As well as enriching his idiom with oriental elements, Puccini had here won through to a new scale of musical thought, to which the love duet of Act 1 bears special witness.

MIDDLE AND LATE YEARS   A lean period followed. Among the subjects taken up and laid aside were Victor Hugo's *Notre Dame de Paris*, Oscar Wilde's unfinished play *A Florentine Tragedy* and Pierre Louÿs's *La femme et le pantin* (later set by Riccardo Zandonai as *Conchita*). At one point Puccini considered a collaboration with Italy's foremost poet, Gabriele D'Annunzio, but that too came to nothing. Of his two librettists, Giacosa died in 1906, while Illica remained for years engaged in drawing up a *Maria Antonietta* which he never finished to the composer's satisfaction. Almost *faute de mieux* Puccini turned to another Belasco play, *The Girl of the Golden West*, with a tougher, more resilient heroine. Work on *La fanciulla del West* was interrupted by a particularly unpleasant domestic crisis. An unfaithful husband, Puccini was suspected by his wife of having an affair with their maidservant, Doria Manfredi. She persecuted Manfredi to such an extent that the girl committed suicide. A subsequent autopsy proved her to be a virgin, whereupon her family sued

Elvira Puccini for gross defamation of character. Ultimately a settlement was reached whereby she escaped a prison sentence, and peace was gradually restored to the Puccini household. But the scandal had resulted in a hiatus of nine months in the composition of *La fanciulla del West*, which finally had its première at the Metropolitan Opera House, New York, in December 1910. To outward appearance it was a triumphant success, but its new harmonic elaboration, combined with a curbing of the lyrical impulse that had marked Puccini's earlier scores, alienated many of the composer's admirers; the opera has never entered the circle of steady favourites.

At the same time Puccini found himself under attack from another quarter. A new generation of Italian composers had arisen, represented by Casella, Pizzetti and Gian Francesco Malipiero, who, in their concern to revive the glories of their country's polyphonic past and with it a long defunct instrumental tradition, set their faces firmly against Italian opera, especially its latest manifestations. Their standard-bearer, the critic Fausto Torrefranca, launched a savage diatribe against the author of *La Bohème* and *Madama Butterfly* under the title *Giacomo Puccini e l'opera internazionale*, which called into question not only his taste but also his musicianship.

Puccini, however, refused to be deflected from his chosen path. His next venture was into the world of Lehár with his operetta-like (though through-composed) *La rondine* (1917, Monte Carlo). A Viennese commission, originally intended for the Carltheater, its composition covered the years of Italy's entry into World War I – another difficult period for Puccini, who was suspected, not without reason, of lacking enthusiasm for the Allied cause. He had refused to join Debussy, Elgar, Mascagni and others in contributing to Hall Caine's *King Albert's Book* in honour of 'brave little Belgium', and for this was ferociously attacked in an open letter by Alphonse Daudet's son Léon. (He later placated French hostility by devoting a year's profits from performances of *Tosca* by the Opéra-Comique to the benefit of the country's wounded.) His own son, Tonio, then in uniform, was likewise a source of anxiety. Nonetheless, he managed to finish *La rondine*, which had its première on neutral soil before reaching Italy. Neither at home nor abroad did it ever enjoy an enduring success. In the meantime Puccini had been working on the long-cherished project of a triple-bill of contrasted one-act operas. Here he enjoyed the benefit of two young librettists of outstanding ability: Giuseppe Adami, his collaborator on *La rondine*, who drew up the text for *Il tabarro* from a Grand Guignol melodrama by Didier Gold, and Giovacchino Forzano, whose *Suor Angelica* and *Gianni Schicchi* were his own invention. The so-called *Trittico* was first given (in Puccini's absence) at the Metropolitan Opera House, New York, in December 1918. Though in subsequent revivals *Suor Angelica* failed to stay the course, all three operas were recognized as showing a new strength and confidence. Puccini's position as Italy's leading opera composer was now unchallenged even by Mascagni (though in 1921 the latter scored a momentary, unexpected triumph with *Il piccolo Marat*). His last efforts were directed towards a large-scale opera which should explore entirely new territory. This was to be *Turandot*, derived from a *fiaba* (fairy-tale) by the 18th-century Venetian playwright Carlo Gozzi. Its gestation was long and difficult; nor did the librettist Adami and his partner Renato Simoni ever succeed in working out to the composer's satisfaction the text of a final duet which would bring about a convincing denouement, with the result that by the time of Puccini's death (in Brussels on 29 November 1924, from heart failure while under surgical treatment for cancer of the throat) the opera was unfinished. In the meantime his status had been confirmed by his nomination as Senator of the Realm.

DRAMATURGY AND MUSICAL STYLE   Puccini stands as the supreme exponent of a style of opera which first became popular following the success of Mascagni's *Cavalleria rusticana* (1890). Often loosely, and indeed misleadingly, labelled 'verismo', it is characterized by a swift, naturalistic action similar to that of a spoken play and a full-blooded romantic rhetoric that owes much to Massenet and something to Wagner. In a letter of 1895 written to Carlo Clausetti of Ricordi, Puccini complained that as early as *Le villi* (1884) he had already established the 'stile mascagnano' but that nobody gave him the credit for it. Musically speaking, his claim was justified. In *Le villi* all the basic traits of the 'giovane scuola' (as

Puccini's generation came to be called) are already present, while *Edgar* shows the establishment of a strongly personal idiom with fingerprints that were to remain constant throughout the composer's career: diatonic melodies without chromatic inflection that move mostly by step while incorporating many a falling 5th, sequences with a heavy subdominant bias, successions of parallel, often unrelated chords, frequent use of added notes and unresolved dissonances, climaxes built on alternating progressions, and a habit of doubling the outer parts with harmonies sandwiched in between. If the style appears relatively narrow, it is sufficiently flexible to absorb in the course of its evolution elements from more advanced contemporaries such as Debussy, Richard Strauss and Stravinsky, as well as those of exotic folk music.

In matters of construction Puccini was far ahead of his Italian rivals, avoiding their tendency to formless rhapsodizing by organizing his acts motivically and even weaving motifs into the fabric of a detachable number (e.g., 'Che gelida manina' in *La bohème* and 'Vissi d'arte' in *Tosca*). At the same time a remarkable capacity for self-renewal, comparable to Verdi's, ensured a steady progress from one opera to the next, sometimes accompanied by a modification of technique. The symphonic tendencies evident in much of *Manon Lescaut* (much of the first act is like an elaborate scherzo) give way in *La bohème* to a more relaxed procedure in which thematic reminiscence and leitmotif play a prominent role – a method which reached its apogee in *Tosca*. It should be noted, however, that Puccini's use of leitmotif was rarely as systematically referential as Wagner's. Ernest Newman's gibe that Puccini often seemed to have forgotten where his motifs had first occurred is beside the point. Over and above their power of recall, Puccini exploited them for their cohesive force and their emotional charge, which may vary according to their dynamic and scoring. In his orchestral perorations (a device derived from Ponchielli) he has been accused of quoting inappropriate themes – Colline's farewell to his overcoat at the end of *La bohème*, 'E lucevan le stelle' for the final curtain of *Tosca*; yet each strikes the right note of personal grief. In *Suor Angelica* not one of the many motifs can be related to a particular person or idea. By that time Puccini had arrived at yet another structural method, involving large musical blocks, each hewn from the same material (this too could be said to have a Wagnerian precedent in Isolde's narration, King Mark's lament for Tristan's betrayal and Pogner's address in Act 1 of *Die Meistersinger*). Such is the organizing principle behind *Il tabarro* and, above all, *Turandot*.

In the domain of stagecraft Puccini remains unsurpassed. Not even Wagner was more concerned than he to integrate music, words and gesture into a single scenic concept, with the result that his operas are virtually director-proof. None of his detailed stage directions can be ignored without detriment to the general effect. As early as *Manon Lescaut* he breached the time-honoured convention of the static *pezzo concertato* with an ensemble of action, namely the roll-call of the prostitutes in Act 3. From then on his massed choral scenes conform to this type, with the sole exception of the consciously operetta-style brindisi ('Beviam al tuo fresco sorriso') of *La rondine*. Following the example set by Bellini in *I puritani* the majority of his heroines are heard before they are seen, so that they are established first and foremost as voices. In *Turandot*, on the other hand, the procedure is no less happily reversed. Several of the later operas show a characteristic scheme whereby the action proceeds through a number of apparently unrelated incidents until at a certain moment the listener is made aware that the central drama has been launched: the entrance of Dick Johnson alias Ramerrez (*La fanciulla del West*), the sighting of the Princess's carriage (*Suor Angelica*) and the point at which Luigi and Giorgetta are alone for the first time (*Il tabarro*). To all this must be added Puccini's rare gift of evoking an ambience, often mixing music with extraneous noise (the bells in *Tosca*, the ship's sirens in *Il tabarro*). Even Debussy, no friend to the contemporary school of Italian opera, once confessed to Paul Dukas that he knew of no one who had described the Paris of the age of Louis-Philippe 'as well as Puccini in *La bohème*'.

ASSESSMENT   Puccini's limitations as an artist were, in a sense, spiritual. His values were those of 'L'italietta', the bourgeois, unadventurous Italy before World War I. 'Great sorrows in little souls' was his watchword, he told Gabriele D'Annunzio; and that alone would have rendered him incapable of matching in music the poet's daring aesthetic flights. His love of tugging the heart-strings led him to favour – though by no means exclusively, as is sometimes implied – the soft, wilting heroines and to wind up almost sadistically the agony of their destruction. That this did not preclude a genuine talent for comedy is demonstrated by parts of *La bohème* and all of *Gianni Schicchi*, but it debarred him from the highest level of tragedy. The wider issues, whether of politics or religion, lay outside his grasp. For him there was no glory beyond the grave. Each of his victims could have echoed Shakespeare's Iras in *Antony and Cleopatra*: 'Finish, good lady; the bright day is done, And we are for the dark'. Hence his refusal to end *Tosca* on the note of facile uplift that marks the conclusion of Giordano's *Andrea Chénier*. Inevitably, when an element of transfiguration was required he was found wanting: a defect that prevented him from finishing *Suor Angelica* satisfactorily and *Turandot* at all.

Puccini still has his detractors, who have expressed themselves as savagely as Torrefranca in 1912. Nevertheless, his hold on the public remains as strong as ever; and it can be safely maintained that, however prejudiced to start with, anyone who has worked practically on his operas has ended with a profound respect for Puccini as musician and man of the theatre.

J.B.

Operas

Le villi
('The Willis')

Opera-ballo in two acts set to a libretto by Ferdinando Fontana after Alphonse Karr's short story *Les Willis*; first performed in Milan, at the Teatro Dal Verme, on 31 May 1884. The revised version was first performed in Turin, at the Teatro Regio, on 26 December 1884.

*

In the Black Forest villagers are celebrating the engagement of Roberto (tenor) and Anna (soprano), daughter of the head forester, Guglielmo (baritone). Roberto is about to leave for Mainz to collect an inheritance. Anna brings him a posy of forget-me-nots to keep him mindful of their vows ('Se come voi piccina'). In their duet 'Tu dall'infanzia mia' he tells her to doubt the existence of God himself rather than his own constancy. All join in a prayer ('Angiol di Dio') to speed him on his way.

At the beginning of Act 2 a verse of poetry describes how Roberto has fallen into the clutches of a siren and forgotten Anna, who died of grief. During an intermezzo ('L'abbandono') her body is borne across the stage behind a gauze curtain to an unseen chorus of mourners. A second intermezzo ('La tregenda'), preceded by more poetry, depicts the dance of the Willis, ghosts of jilted maidens. Outside his cottage Guglielmo grieves for his daughter and inveighs against her faithless lover ('Anima santa della figlia mia'). Roberto returns penniless and devoured by remorse, recalling his love for Anna ('Torna ai felici dì'). The Willis appear, among them Anna, who taunts him with his treachery. They dance until Roberto falls dead at her feet.

*

Le villi, Puccini's first stage work, was originally entered for a competition for a one-act opera announced in 1883 by the publisher Sonzogno in his periodical *Il teatro illustrato*; but it failed to achieve even an honourable mention. However, friends and well-wishers, among them Boito, subscribed to a performance which took place under the baton of Achille Panizza with Rosina Caponetti (Anna), Antonio D'Andrade (Roberto) and Erminio Pelz (Guglielmo) and an orchestra that included Pietro Mascagni among the double basses. The reception was sufficiently encouraging for Ricordi to purchase the score. He persuaded Puccini and Fontana to enlarge the opera (originally described as a 'leggenda in due quadri') into its present form, adding Anna's cavatina in Act 1 and a dramatic scena for Roberto in Act 2, inserting the invisible chorus into the first inter-mezzo and converting what had originally been an aria finale for the soprano into a duet for her and the tenor. The final addition was the tenor *romanza* 'Torna ai felici dì', composed during the course of a revival at La Scala, Milan in January 1885 under Franco Faccio with Romilda Pantaleoni (who later created Verdi's Desdemona) as the heroine. Further modifications followed in the editions of 1888 and 1892, the latter being the one in general use today.

Like many a beginner's work *Le villi* shows a number of influ-ences, from Ponchielli and Catalani (notably in the tenor *romanza*) to Gounod and Bizet in the dance movements, Massenet in the solos, and even the Weber of *Der Freischütz* in the final scene. At the same time Puccini's individual voice can be heard in the atmospheric prelude whose opening theme, a motif that will connote Roberto's vow of fidelity, is taken from a *romanza*, *Melanconia* (1881), since lost; in Anna's cavatina and subsequent duet with Roberto – in the variety of phrase-structure and flexible articulation of the verbal text; in the preghiera, based on an earlier song, *Salve del ciel regina*; in the first intermezzo, with its languishing melodies that incline towards the subdominant, its prolonged suspensions and yearning insistence on variants of the dominant 9th; and in the abundance of thematic reminiscence towards the end of the work. The second intermezzo, a miniature 'Walkürenritt', is the only instrumental piece in a Puccini opera that will bear transplantation from its original context. But for all its vitality *Le villi* is not so much a drama as a story. There is no interplay of character, no one to react to Guglielmo's grief or Roberto's remorse; hence the opera's virtual exclusion from the Puccini canon. On the rare occasions when it is performed the snatches of poetry are declaimed by a narrator; but it would seem that they were intended merely to be read by the audience.

J.B.

Edgar

Dramma lirico in three acts (originally four acts) set to a libretto by
Ferdinando Fontana after Alfred de Musset's dramatic poem *La
coupe et les lèvres*; first performed in Milan's Teatro alla Scala, on
21 April 1889. The definitive version was first performed in Buenos
Aires at the Teatro de la Opera, on 8 July 1905.

Puccini's first full-length opera, commissioned by Ricordi to a
libretto by the author of *Le villi*, *Edgar* was first given under Franco
Faccio with Gregorio Gabrielesco as Edgar (tenor), Pio Marini as
Gualtiero (bass), Antonio Magini-Coletti as Frank (baritone), Aurelia
Cataneo-Caruson as Fidelia (soprano) and Romilda Pantaleoni as
Tigrana (soprano).

Edgar was coolly received and ran for only three performances. Of
various revivals projected over the next two years the only one to
materialize took place at Puccini's native town, Lucca, where it
enjoyed great success. Nonetheless the composer decided to suppress
the last act, grafting the sensational denouement on to Act 3, transferring the prelude in shortened form to the beginning of Act 1 and
assigning some of Fidelia's music to Tigrana, now a mezzo-soprano,
in Act 2. Further modifications followed, including the suppression
of the prelude, leading to the definitive version of 1905, first
performed in Buenos Aires, conducted by Leopoldo Mugnone with
Giovanni Zenatello in the title role.

*

The opera is set in Flanders in 1302 and Act 1 takes place in a village
square. Edgar, asleep outside his house, is awakened by Fidelia, who
gives him a sprig of almond blossom. The Moorish Tigrana mocks
the young man's infatuation with an innocent village maiden and
reminds him that he once entertained very different desires. When
Fidelia's brother, the love-lorn Frank, arrives Tigrana repulses him
with scorn, leaving him to lament his enslavement to a woman so
base ('Questo amor, vergogna mia'). The villagers assemble for a
church service, during which Tigrana scandalizes the congregation

with a cruel, implicitly blasphemous song, 'Tu il cuor mi strazi'. They threaten to attack her, but she is defended by Edgar, who sets fire to his house and declares that he will leave the village for ever with her. Their way is barred by Frank. The two men draw their swords, as Fidelia and her father Gualtiero arrive. All express their dismay in a Ponchiellian *pezzo concertato*, after which Edgar drags Tigrana away with him, having first wounded Frank in a duel.

Act 2 takes place on the terrace of a magnificent palace. Edgar regrets his new life of debauchery and thinks longingly of Fidelia ('O soave vision'), while Tigrana vainly tries to re-awaken his desire for her. A troop of soldiers passes, led by Frank. Ignoring Tigrana's pleas Edgar decides to join his former antagonist and redeem his sins in the service of his country.

At the beginning of Act 3 a military funeral is in progress on the battlements of a fortress near Courtray. The soldiers pray for the soul of Edgar, their valiant captain, whom they believe to have fallen in battle. Behind the coffin stand Frank and a monk whose face is concealed beneath his cowl. Also present are Gualtiero and Fidelia, who mourns the death of her only love ('Addio, mio dolce amor'). Frank begins the funeral oration but is interrupted by the monk who reminds the bystanders of Edgar's past misdeeds and so works them up into a fury against his memory. Fidelia defends him as one whose heart is pure and whose sins were merely those of youth ('Nel villaggio d'Edgar'). The people retire shamefacedly. Tigrana enters in deep mourning to pray at Edgar's coffin. In a comic terzetto ('Bella signora, il pianto sciupa gli occhi') Frank and the monk bribe her with the offer of jewels to denounce her lover before the returning crowd as a traitor to his country. The people rush to tear open the coffin, but all they find inside is a suit of armour. The monk uncovers his face to reveal Edgar. He embraces Fidelia and declares that he has been reborn; whereupon Fidelia steals up to her rival and stabs her to the heart.

*

Edgar was first conceived as a grand opera on a Meyerbeerian scale (though without ballet), including a virtuoso role for a dramatic prima donna in the person of Tigrana, modelled partly on Carmen. In revising the opera Puccini eliminated much that was turgid and uncharacteristic; but he also compounded the faults of the dramatic scheme, reducing it to an unexplained succession of bizarre situations. Nowhere does Wagner's gibe about 'effects without causes' seem more apposite. Musically, however, the level of craftsmanship is remarkably high and the crystallization of a personal style already far advanced. Some of the material is re-elaborated from earlier, non-theatrical works, notably the so-called *Messa di gloria* (1880), the *Preludio* in A for orchestra (1882), an *Adagio* for string quartet (1882), the *Capriccio sinfonico* (1883) and the song *Storiella d'amore* (1883). Among the various recurring themes Tigrana's motif has something of the brutality that would later characterize Scarpia in *Tosca*. Other Puccinian features include successions of parallel chords, added notes (especially the 'frozen' sixth) and a fondness for floating a purely diatonic melody on a pattern of unresolved dissonances (ex.1). Part of the duet for Fidelia and Edgar in the discarded fourth act was used again in *Tosca* ('Amaro sol per te'), where, curiously, the harmonic clashes are milder than in the original context.

Alone of Puccini's operas *Edgar* has never been translated into another language. Puccini himself, ever ready to defend his less fortunate offspring such as *La rondine* and *Suor Angelica*, showed no retrospective affection for this one. On a vocal score sent to his friend Sybil Seligman he defaced the title thus: E Dio ti Gu A Rda da quest'-opera ('And may God preserve you from this opera'). However, Toscanini conducted the Act 3 'Requiem' at the composer's funeral in Milan Cathedral on 3 December 1924.

J.B.

Manon Lescaut

Drama lirico in four acts set to a libretto by Domenico Oliva and Luigi Illica after Antoine-François Prévost's novel *L'histoire du chevalier des Grieux et de Manon Lescaut*; first performed in Turin, at the Teatro Regio, on 1 February 1893 (revised version, Milan, Teatro alla Scala, 7 February 1894).

The first performance was conducted by Alessandro Pomè with Cesira Ferrani (Manon), Achille Moro (Lescaut), Giuseppe Cremonini (des Grieux) and Alessandro Polonini (Geronte).

Manon Lescaut	soprano
Lescaut *her brother, Sergeant of the Royal Guards*	baritone
The Chevalier des Grieux	tenor
Geronte de Revoir	bass
Edmondo	tenor
The Innkeeper	bass
A Singer	mezzo-soprano
The Dancing Master	tenor
A Lamplighter	tenor
Sergeant of the Royal Archers	bass
A Naval Captain	bass

Singers, old beaux and abbés, girls, townsfolk, students, courtesans, archers and sailors

Setting France and America during the second half of the 18th century

Puccini's first two operas, *Le villi* (1884) and *Edgar* (1889) had little impact on the general public although they did not escape the notice of critics. His third, *Manon Lescaut*, however, triumphantly vindicated his publisher Giulio Ricordi's faith in him. Of all Puccini's operas *Manon Lescaut* had the most tormented genesis. His publisher Ricordi tried to dissuade him from a subject which had already achieved great popularity in Massenet's setting of 1884, as yet unperformed in Italy.

Puccini remained firm in his decision to undertake it, declaring that 'Manon is a heroine I believe in and therefore she cannot fail to win the hearts of the public. Why shouldn't there be two operas about her? A woman like Manon can have more than one lover.' Dissatisfied with the bizarre pseudophilosophical pretensions of Ferdinando Fontana, who had written the librettos for his previous operas, Puccini first turned to the playwright Marco Praga as a possible librettist. But Praga had never attempted an opera libretto before and insisted on bringing in the young poet Domenico Oliva, with whom he had already collaborated on a literary and artistic journal, to do the versification.

Both authors were contracted by Ricordi during the summer of 1889. By the beginning of the next year they had produced a libretto in four acts set respectively in Amiens, in the lovers' humble apartment in Paris, in Geronte's town house and in the Louisiana desert where Manon dies. Puccini professed himself satisfied and managed to complete the first act by March 1890. But by June he was complaining that the libretto was driving him to despair and that it would have to be re-done. He particularly wanted an entire scene at the end of Act 3 showing the embarkation at Le Havre. Rather than alter his original scheme Praga preferred to bow out. Ricordi then turned to Ruggero Leoncavallo, who drafted out a new scheme for Act 2, leaving Oliva to fill out the lines; then he too retired from the project, owing to pressure of other work. Finally, in autumn 1891 Luigi Illica was called in to overhaul the entire text in accordance with Puccini's requirements. He re-worked the scene at Le Havre into its present form, adding the song of the Lamplighter, while Giulio Ricordi contributed the quatrain in which the ship's captain agrees to take Des Grieux aboard. Puccini himself supplied 11 unmetrical lines for the duet between Lescaut and Manon in Geronte's town house; a further two were provided by Leoncavallo for the conclusion of Des Grieux' solo in the same scene. Some time during the summer of 1892 the original Act 2 was dropped altogether and replaced by what had until then been Act 3 part 1, now suitably expanded. Thus the embarkation scene became a separate act, prefaced by an intermezzo. By this time Oliva no longer wanted to be associated with the opera, but as much of his work exists in the finished product,

Illica tactfully withheld his own name from the title-page, so that the published libretto remains to this day without an attribution. Later Oliva maintained that the fourth act was exactly as he had originally written it. The score was finished in October 1892, Act 3 being completed last. Puccini, as he often did, drew on previous material: the Agnus Dei from his student piece, the so-called *Messa di gloria* (1880) for the 'madrigal' of Act 2; the student exercise *Mentìa l'avviso* (1883) for the melody of Des Grieux' aria 'Donna non vidi mai'; a minuet for string quartet (1884) speeded up for the opera's opening; and the elegy *Crisantemi* (1890), also for quartet, for certain moments in Act 3 and Act 4.

As La Scala was occupied at the time with rehearsals for Verdi's *Falstaff*, Ricordi chose the Teatro Regio Turin, for the première. *Manon Lescaut* was Puccini's first and only uncontested triumph, acclaimed by critics and public alike; its success meant that his financial problems were permanently solved. Ricordi took advantage of the favourable reception to link its hire with that of *Falstaff*, so that neither opera could be given without the other. Before the published vocal score appeared Puccini made, at Illica's suggestion, a radical change to the finale of Act 1, replacing a conventional *pezzo concertato*, based on the melody of 'Donna non vidi mai', by an exchange between Lescaut and Geronte and a reprise of the melody of Des Grieux' 'Tra voi belle' entrusted to Edmondo and the students. The new finale was first performed on 7 February 1894 at La Scala, where the cast included Olga Olghini (Manon), Tieste Wilmant (Lescaut), Vittorio Arimondi (Geronte) and the original Des Grieux, Cremonini. The London première (Covent Garden, 14 May 1894), with Olghini (Manon), Antonio Pini-Corsi (Lescaut) and Umberto Beduschi (Des Grieux), prompted Bernard Shaw to hail Puccini as Verdi's most probable heir among Italian composers, noting that 'the domain of Italian opera is enlarged by an annexation of German territory'. The opera established itself at the Metropolitan, New York (18 January 1907), with Lina Cavalieri (Manon), Antonio Scotti (Lescaut) and Enrico Caruso (Des Grieux). Outstanding exponents of the title role have included Lucrezia Bori, who introduced the opera to Paris in 1910, and Lotte Lehmann, who sang it in Vienna in 1923 with Alfred Piccaver as Des Grieux.

Puccini continued to modify *Manon Lescaut*, in particular omitting for many years the heroine's aria in Act 4, 'Sola, perduta, abbandonata'. He finally reinstated it with a slightly altered ending for the 30th anniversary performance, given at La Scala (1 February 1923) under Toscanini with Juanita Caracciolo in the title role. Toscanini himself suggested certain alterations to the scoring, all of which have since been incorporated in the current version of the opera.

*

ACT 1   *A public square in Amiens*   Outside an inn soldiers, students and townsfolk are enjoying the fine summer evening. Edmondo leads the company in a 'madrigal' ('Ave sera gentil'). The students welcome Des Grieux, who addresses a group of girls with ironical gallantry ('Tra voi belle, brune o blonde'). The young Manon arrives on the stage coach from Arras accompanied by her brother Lescaut and Geronte, who orders lodgings for the night. The cynical Lescaut, aware of the older man's interest in his sister, is happy to collude in his plans for her. The two men go into the inn. The crowd disperse leaving Manon alone with Des Grieux. She tells him that she is bound for a convent, but agrees to meet him later. When she has left, Des Grieux pours out his feelings in the soliloquy 'Donna non vidi mai'. Edmondo overhears Geronte summoning a carriage to leave for Paris within the hour and warns Des Grieux. He and Manon sing a love-duet ('Vedete? io son fedele') before making their escape in the carriage. Lescaut assures the mortified Geronte that his sister will soon need a rich protector as Des Grieux has no money.

ACT 2   *An elegant salon in Geronte's house*   Manon, installed as Geronte's mistress, is in the hands of her hairdresser when Lescaut enters. She asks for news of Des Grieux, recalling nostalgically the humble apartment in which they were happy together and contrasting it with her present luxurious surroundings ('In quelle trine morbide'). Lescaut tells her that he has turned the young man into a gambler, so that he may win enough money to provide her with the luxury she cannot do without. A group of singers perform a madrigal in her honour ('Sulla vetta tu del monte'), after which Lescaut goes to fetch Des Grieux. Geronte arrives with friends who offer bouquets and trinkets. A dancing master teaches her the minuet. Manon takes leave of the company with a brief 'pastoral' ('L'ora, o Tirsi, è vaga e bella'), promising to join them later on the boulevards. Des Grieux appears at the door. In their duet ('Tu, tu, amore') he begins by reproaching her, but she soon overcomes his resistance and Geronte returns to find them in each other's arms. Manon parries his ironic thrusts by holding a mirror to his face. He retires, threatening that they will meet again. The lovers prepare to flee; but Manon is sad at having to relinquish so much wealth, as Des Grieux observes with dismay ('Ah, Manon, mi tradisce il too folle pensier'). To a brisk orchestral fugato Lescaut bursts in to tell them that Geronte is on his way back with the city guards. Manon's insistence on gathering up the jewels causes a fatal delay. As Geronte and the guards enter the jewels spill out of her cloak, and she is arrested for theft.

ACT 3   *Le Havre, a square near the harbour*   An intermezzo based on previously heard themes covers the time of Manon's imprisonment and the journey to the French port. As a woman of loose character she is housed in a barracks with prostitutes awaiting deportation to America. Lescaut plans to procure her escape by bribing a guard. As Manon appears at a grille, she and Des Grieux exchange words of love and hope while a lamplighter passes by on his rounds. A shot is heard, indicating that Lescaut's plan has miscarried. One by one the prostitutes and Manon are taken to the ship, while a sergeant-at-arms calls their names and the crowd comment on the appearance of each. Des Grieux prevails upon the ship's captain to take him aboard in a solo, 'Guardate, pazzo son, guardate', and with a reminiscence of the Act 2 duet, he falls into Manon's arms.

ACT 4   *A vast desert near the outskirts of New Orleans*   Manon, in flight with Des Grieux from the son of the French governor, is at the end of her strength. She sends Des Grieux to look for shelter for the night, then breaks out in an agonized lament, 'Sola, perduta, abbandonata'. Des Grieux returns to find her dying.

*

Manon Lescaut placed Puccini firmly in the front rank of contemporary composers. Bernard Shaw correctly drew attention to the symphonic element in Act 1, while the *grand tableau* in the third act represents something new in Italian musical dramaturgy – *a pezzo concertato* in which time is never frozen. No less remarkable is Puccini's skill in depicting the dawning of young love, first with an orchestral anticipation of Des Grieux' aria 'Donna non vidi mai', then in the course of the duet 'Vedete? io son fedele', in which shy conversational exchanges gradually flower into an ecstatic lyricism. Thematic recurrence is used with a new flexibility, exemplified by the various transformations undergone by the motif associated with the heroine. At moments of high emotion *Manon Lescaut* comes nearer the Wagner of *Tristan* than do any of Puccini's other operas.

On the debit side, the elimination of the lovers' Parisian idyll not only leaves an awkward gap in the action but also precludes a full portrayal of Manon's character. Indeed, as late as 1903 a letter to Illica, undated but obviously written several years later, shows Puccini toying with the notion of an additional act showing the lovers living happily together in Paris. The chief difficulty lay in finding a sufficiently original ending. Also unsatisfactory is the concentration of all the gaiety into Acts 1 and 2 and all the gloom into Acts 3 and 4. But any such weaknesses are amply made good by the abundance of youthful vitality, which has enabled Puccini's opera to hold its own against Massenet's technically more adroit setting of the same subject.

J.B.

La bohème
('Bohemian Life')

Opera in four acts set to a libretto by Giuseppe Giacosa and Luigi Illica after Henry Murger's novel *Scènes de la vie de bohème*; first performed in Turin at the Teatro Regio, on 1 February 1896.

The principals at the première were Cesira Ferrani (Mimì), Camilla Pasini (Musetta), Evan Gorga (Rodolfo), Michele Mazzini (Colline) and Antonio Pini-Corsi (Schaunard); the conductor was Toscanini.

Rodolfo *a poet*	tenor
Mimì *a seamstress*	soprano
Marcello *a painter*	baritone
Schaunard *a musician*	baritone
Colline *a philosopher*	bass
Musetta *a singer*	soprano
Benoit *their landlord*	bass
Alcindoro *a state councillor*	bass
Parpignol *a toy vendor*	tenor
A customs offical	bass

Students, working girls, townsfolk, shopkeepers, streetvendors, soldiers, waiters and children

Setting Paris, about 1830

Puccini's intention to base an opera on Murger's picaresque novel appears to date from the winter of 1892–3, shortly before the première of *Manon Lescaut*. Almost at once it involved him in a controversy in print with Leoncavallo, who in the columns of his publisher's periodical *Il secolo* (20 March 1893) claimed precedence in the subject, maintaining that he had already approached the artists whom he had in mind and that Puccini knew this perfectly well. Puccini rebutted the accusation in a letter (dated the following day) to *Il corriere della sera* (drafted by Illica, but signed by the composer) and at the same time welcomed the prospect of competing with his rival and allowing the public to judge the winner.

Scènes de la vie de bohème existed both as a novel, originally published in serial form, and as a play written in collaboration with Théodore Parrière. There were good reasons why neither Puccini nor Leoncavallo should have availed themselves of the latter, whose plot in places runs uncomfortably close to that of *La traviata* (Mimì is persuaded to leave Rodolfo by her lover's wealthy uncle, who uses the same arguments as Verdi's Germont). As the novel was in the public domain Ricordi's attempt to secure exclusive rights to it on Puccini's behalf were unsuccessful. Work proceeded slowly, partly because Puccini had not yet definitely renounced his idea of an opera based on Giovanni Verga's *La lupa* and partly because he spent much of the next two years travelling abroad to supervise performances of *Manon Lescaut* in various European cities. By June 1893 Illica had already completed a prose scenario of which Giacosa, who was given the task of putting it into verse, entirely approved. Here the drama was articulated in four acts and five scenes: the Bohemians' garret and the Café Momus (Act 1), the Barrière d'Enfer (Act 2), the courtyard of Musetta's house (Act 3) and Mimì's death in the garret (Act 4). Giacosa completed the versification by the end of June and submitted it to Puccini and Ricordi, who felt sufficiently confident to announce in the columns of the *Gazzetta musicale di Milano* that the libretto was ready for setting to music. He was premature. Giacosa was required to revise the courtyard and Barrière scenes, a labour which he found so uncongenial that in October he offered – not for the last time – to withdraw from the project; however, he was persuaded by Ricordi to remain.

At a conference with his publisher and the librettists during the winter of 1893–4, Puccini insisted on jettisoning the courtyard scene and with it Mimì's desertion of Rodolfo for a rich 'Viscontino' only to return to the poet in the final act. The librettists strongly objected, but Illica finally proposed a solution whereby the last act, instead of opening with Mimì already on her deathbed as originally planned, would begin with a scene for the four Bohemians similar to that of Act 1, while Mimì's absence would be the subject of an aria by

Rodolfo. The aria became a duet, but otherwise Illica's scheme was adopted in all essentials. Other revisions outlined by Illica and filled out by Giacosa during 1894 included the two self-descriptions of Rodolfo and Mimì' in Act 1 and their duet 'O soave fanciulla'. At the time the Café Momus scene was still envisaged as a 'concertato finale'to Act 1; nor is it clear precisely when it was made into a separate act. At one point Illica wished to eliminate it altogether, but Puccini stoutly defended the Latin quarter 'the way I described it . . . with Musetta's scene which *I* invented'. His own doubts, curiously, concerned the Barriére d'Enfer, a scene that owes nothing to Murger and which the composer felt gave insufficient scope for musical development. His suggestion that they replace it with another episode from the novel was curtly refused by Illica.

Having finally decided to abandon *La lupa* in the summer of 1894 Puccini began the composition of *La bohème*. From then on the librettists' work consisted mostly of elimination, extending even to details on whose inclusion Puccini had originally insisted, such as a drinking song and a diatribe against women, both allocated to Schaunard. The score was finished on 10 December 1895.

Since La Scala was now under the management of the publisher Edoardo Sonzogno, who made a point of excluding all Ricordi scores from the repertory, the première was fixed for the Teatro Regio, Turin (where *Manon Lescaut* had received its première in 1893). The public response was mixed: favourable to Acts 1 and 4, less so to the others. Most of the critics saw in the opera a falling-off from *Manon Lescaut* in the direction of triviality. But nothing could stop its rapid circulation. A performance at the Teatro Argentina, Rome, under Edoardo Mascheroni (23 February) introduced Rosina Storchio as Musetta, a role in which she later excelled. A revival at the Politeama Garibaldi, Palermo (24 April) under Leopoldo Mugnone included for the first time the Act 2 episode where Mimì shows off her bonnet. On this occasion Rodolfo and Mimì were played by Edoardo Garbin and Adelina Stehle (the original young lovers of Verdi's *Falstaff*), who did much to make *La bohème* popular in southern Italy in the years that followed. Outside Italy most premières of La bohème were given in smaller theatres and in the vernacular of the country. In Paris it was first given in 1898 by the Opéra-Comique, as *La vie de bohème*, and achieved its 1000th performance there in 1951. After a performance at Covent Garden by the visiting Carl Rosa company in 1897 *La bohème* first established itself in the repertory of the Royal Italian Opera on 1 July 1899 with a cast that included Nellie Melba (Mimì), Zélie de Lussan (Musetta), Alessandro Bonci (Rodolfo), Mario Ancona (Marcello) and Marcel Journet (Colline). From then on its fortunes in Britain and America were largely associated with Melba, who was partnered, among others, by Fernando de Lucia, John McCormack, Giovanni Martinelli and, most memorably of all, Enrico Caruso. Today *La bohème* remains, with *Tosca* and *Madama Butterfly*, one of the central pillars of the Italian repertory; its centenary performances in February 1996 confirmed its perennial appeal.

*

ACT 1 *A garret overlooking the snow-covered roofs of Paris; Christmas eve* The act opens in a conversational style based on two motifs, one instrumental, the other vocal. The first, taken from the central section of Puccini's *Capriccio sinfonico* (1883), is associated with Marcello and the Bohemians generally; the second, to the words 'Nei cieli bigi', derives from sketches for the abandoned *La lupa* and belongs to Rodolfo. Both men are chafing at the cold. Marcello suggests chopping up a chair for firewood; but Rodolfo prefers to burn the five-act drama on which he has been working. Colline enters to find the hearth ablaze. Just as the fire is about to die a brisk orchestral theme heralds the arrival of Schaunard accompanied by two boys carrying logs and victuals. While his three friends take charge of their disposal Schaunard explains his sudden wealth. He had been employed by a rich milord to play to a neighbour's noisy parrot until it dropped dead. He charmed the chambermaid into giving him some parsley which he fed to the parrot, who promptly died; hence his own reward. The Bohemians decide to celebrate by dining out in the Latin Quarter (and here the orchestra adumbrates a motif of parallel triads which will connote the Café Momus), when there is a knock at the door. It is their landlord, Benoit, come to demand the rent. They receive him cordially and ply him with wine together with much flattery regarding his amorous exploits; when he waxes indiscreet over his wife's ugliness and ill-nature they pretend to be shocked and throw him out. They depart for the Café Momus, leaving Rodolfo to finish writing an article before joining them. Soon there is another, more timid knock on the door. It is Mimì, their neighbour, whose candle has gone out. Rodolfo ushers her into a chair as she is clearly ailing and revives her with a glass of wine. She is about to leave when she discovers that she has dropped her key. Together they look for it. Rodolfo finds it and slips it into his pocket; then his hand touches Mimì's, prompting his aria 'Che gelida manina' ('Your tiny hand is frozen'), which incorporates a reminiscence of his own motif. Mimì replies with a modest story of her life, 'Mi chiamano Mimì', whose opening strain will serve as her own identifying motif. The voices of the Bohemians are heard below urging Rodolfo to make haste. He replies that he is not alone. He then turns to see Mimì bathed in a shaft of moonlight and the act concludes with their duet 'O soave fanciulla', which is partly a reprise of 'Che gelida manina'.

ACT 2   *A crossroads with the Café Momus to one side*   Tables are set out on the pavement, between which waiters hurry to and fro. To the 'Momus' motif, resplendent on brass, vendors from nearby shops hawk their wares. Schaunard disputes with a shopkeeper, Rodolfo takes Mimì to buy a bonnet, Colline exults over the purchase of a book and Marcello ogles the passing girls. He, Colline and Schaunard carry out a table from the cafe and sit down at it, to the annoyance of other clients, and Rodolfo presents Mimì to his friends. Mimì expresses delight in her new bonnet. To a vigorous theme in 9/8, one of whose phrases will be associated with her throughout the opera, Musetta makes a spectacular entrance, followed by her latest 'protector', the state councillor Alcindoro. Seeing Marcello, the lover to whom she always returns, she stages a scene for his benefit. She torments Alcindoro by complaining about the service, smashing a plate and then bursting into song ('Quando me'n vo'), a shameless piece of exhibitionism which forms the musical basis of an ensemble. Finally, she gets rid of her escort by pretending that her shoes are hurting and sending him off to buy another pair. Then she falls into Marcello's arms, to the delight of the bystanders. The waiter arrives to settle accounts. As a military tattoo passes by Musetta tells the Bohemians to add their bill to hers. They leave as Alcindoro returns with the shoes and is presented with the bill.

ACT 3 *The Barrière d'Enfer* A descending motif of parallel 5ths on flute and harp evokes a cold winter's dawn. From the nearby tavern come the sounds of revelry. The toll-gate keepers admit street cleaners and then milkmaids. Mimì enters to a reminiscence of her motif, broken off by a fit of coughing. She inquires for Marcello and when he appears pours out her heart to him. Rodolfo has ruined their life together with his unreasonable jealousy. As Marcello attempts to comfort her Rodolfo comes out of the inn. Mimì hides and overhears him telling Marcello that he intends to leave her because she is a flirt; then under pressure from Marcello he admits the real reason for their separation; she is dying of consumption and he is unable to provide for her. This revelation is couched in an elegiac terzettino which forms the dramatic crux of the act. Here Puccini uses for the first time a device that served him in the future to depict painful situations: an insistent alternation of minor chords and dissonances over which the voice declaims in monotones. Mimì reveals her presence. Marcello, hearing Musetta's brazen laugh, hurries into the tavern, and Mimì takes a sad farewell of her lover in an arietta interwoven with musical reminiscences ('Donde lieta uscì'). In a final quartet, whose melody is taken directly from Puccini's song 'Sole e amore' (1888), Mimì and Rodolfo decide after all to remain together until the spring, and Musetta and Marcello quarrel furiously.

ACT 4 *The garret, several weeks later* Rodolfo and Marcello are once more at their work, but their thoughts stray to their absent sweethearts ('Ah, Mimì, tu più non torni'). They are joined by Schaunard and Colline bearing meagre provisions. There follows a scene of forced high spirits and horseplay, interrupted by the arrival of Musetta with the dying Mimì. Rodolfo assists her to the bed; Musetta gives her earrings to Marcello, telling him to buy medicine and to send for a doctor; she herself will buy a muff for Mimì's cold hands. Colline bids a mournful farewell to his overcoat which he intends to pawn so as to help the dying girl, in an arietta ('Vecchia zimarra'), he then leaves with Schaunard. During their final duet ('Son partiti? Fingero di dormire') the lovers recall their first meeting, to appropriate musical quotations. The others return, Musetta bringing the muff, pretending that Rodolfo has paid for it; Mimì sinks silently into her death, of which Rodolfo becomes aware only after a burst of agonized questioning (spoken, not sung), answered by the orchestra with a thunderous peroration that combines the operning of 'Son partiti' with the closing bars of 'Vecchia Zimarra' – one of the most tear-jerking of operatic endings.

*

In their preface to the printed libretto Giacosa and Illica claimed to have made their heroine a composite of Murger's Mimì and Francine. In fact she is based almost entirely on Francine, a marginal character in the novel who appears with her lover, the sculptor Jacques, in one chapter only ('Francine's muff') in total isolation from the other Bohemians. Unlike his pert, wilful Mimì, Murger conceived Francine in purely romantic terms – all innocence and fragility. By taking Francine as a model for their Mimì the librettists allowed Puccini not only to distinguish her musically from Musetta, as Leoncavallo was never able to do, but also to achieve that perfect balance of realism and romanticism, of comedy and pathos which makes La bohème, on its own level, one of the most satisfying works in the operatic repertory.

There is a retreat here both from the 'symphonism' that marked Act 1 of Manon Lescaut as well as from the unrestrained emotionalism of its last two acts. Mimì, an archetypally fragile Puccinian heroine, tugs at the heart-strings mostly by a subdued pathos; only once in Act 3 does she burst out in an agony of soul ('O buon Marcello, aiuto!'). La bohème establishes a first-act design, already outlined in Manon Lescaut, which served Puccini for all the operas of his middle period, namely a lively opening with much variety of incident that eventually broadens out into a calm love-duet. Throughout, the harmonic idiom is bolder yet more subtle than in Puccini's previous operas (the triads of the Café Momus theme would not disgrace the Stravinsky of 15 years later). His ability to conjure up a particular ambience is nowhere shown to better advantage than at the start of Act 3, with its suggestion of falling snowflakes conveyed by a succession of open 5ths on flutes and harp over a cello line pedal. Debussy, who disliked the works of the 'giovane scuola', is reported to have said to Falla that he knew of no one who had described the Paris of that time better than Puccini.

J.B.

Tosca

Melodramma in three acts set to a libretto by Giuseppe Giacosa and Luigi Illica after Victorien Sardou's play *La Tosca*; first performed in Rome, at the Teatro Costanzi, on 14 January 1900.

   The first cast included Hariclea Darclée (Tosca), Emilio de Marchi (Cavaradossi) and Eugenio Giraldoni (Scarpia); the conductor was Leopoldo Mugnone.

Floria Tosca *a celebrated singer*	soprano
Mario Cavaradossi *a painter*	tenor
Baron Scarpia *Chief of Police*	baritone
Cesare Angelotti *former Consul of the Roman republic*	bass
A Sacristan	bass
Spoletta *a police agent*	tenor
Sciarrone *a gendarme*	bass
A Gaoler	bass
A Sherpherd-boy	alto
Roberti *the executioner*	silent role

Soldiers, police agents, noblemen and women, towns-folk, artisans

Silent: cardinal, judge, scribe, officer, sergeant

Setting Rome, June 1800

Puccini owed his flair for discovering the operatic possibilities of plays to his early familiarity with a wide range of dramatic literature, an to the strong tradition of spoken drama in his birthplace of Lucca. In May 1889, less than a month after the première of *Edgar*, Puccini wrote to the publisher Ricordi begging him to obtain Sardou's permission to set his play, 'since in this *Tosca* I see the opera that I need: one without excessive proportions or a decorative spectacle; nor is it the kind that calls for a superabundance of music' – by which he meant that it did not conform to the genre of 'grand opera' which had been in vogue in Italy since the 1870s. For the time being matters went no further and Puccini turned his attention to other subjects. In 1895, however, he saw the play performed in Florence with Sarah Bernhardt (for whom it was written) in the title role. The following year, with *La bohème* behind him, he returned to his idea. Unfortunately Sardou had by now granted the rights to Alberto Franchetti, and Luigi Illica had already written him a libretto, to which Verdi had given his unqualified approval. However, Illica and Ricordi had no difficulty in persuading Franchetti, who was dissatisfied with it, to relinquish it and so leave the field open for their favourite composer. As usual the versification was entrusted to Giuseppe Giacosa, who to begin with was against the project. There was too much plot, he argued, and too little room for lyrical expansion, and, as so often, he continually threatened to withdraw from the partnership. However, by the beginning of 1898 Puccini had the entire libretto in his hands and was able to begin work on the first act. In June of that year he visited Sardou in Paris, who encumbered him with various suggestions ('a fine fellow', Puccini wrote, 'all life and fire and full of historico-topo-panoramic inexactitudes'). Sardou gave his blessing to the libretto, however; and Puccini himself considered it an improvement on the original play.

As always, Puccini was much concerned with authenticity of detail. His friend Father Pietro Panichelli supplied him with information regarding the plainsong melody to which the *Te Deum* was sung in Roman churches, the correct order of the cardinal's procession and the costumes of the Swiss Guard. From Meluzzi, an elderly musician in the employ of the Vatican, he learnt the exact pitch of the great bell of St Peter's; and he made a special journey to Rome to hear for himself the effect of the matins bells from the ramparts of the Castel Sant'Angelo. The Roman poet Luigi Zanazzo provided a suitable text for the song of the Shepherd-boy featured in the prelude to Act 3, the last piece to be composed. By the time the opera was completed in October 1899 two important changes had been made to the libretto. In Act 2 Puccini rejected an aria sung by Cavaradossi under torture which developed into a quartet with Tosca, the Judge and Spoletta, on the grounds that it reverted to the static *pezzo concertato* convention of a bygone age. Likewise he would have none of a 'Farewell to Art and Life' to be sung by the painter as he awaits execution, despite Verdi's avowed admiration for it. Instead he insisted on a lover's anguished lament built around the words 'Muoio disperato'. And, as usual, after much argument with his librettists, he had his way. More disturbing was a letter from Giulio Ricordi complaining of the lack of a transcendental love duet in Act 3 which should form the climax of the drama – doubtless he had in mind the concluding scene of Giordano's highly successful *Andrea Chénier* (1896). Ricordi found the existing dialogue between the lovers intolerably perfunctory, and he regretted the musical quotation from the original version of *Edgar* ('Where indeed is the Puccini of noble, warm and vigorous inspiration?'). The composer stood firm. Tosca, he maintained, would be far too preoccupied with the outcome of events to be able to indulge in a time-wasting effusion. In this, as so often, his theatrical instinct had not betrayed him.

Presumably it was the opera's Roman setting that led Ricordi to arrange the première in the Italian capital. The sets were by Adolfo Hohenstein, chief stage designer of La Scala, and the production was in the hands of Tito Ricordi, Giulio's son. Although the critical reception was mixed – several reviewers took exception to the brutality of the plot – the opera ran for 20 evenings to packed houses. Its success was confirmed two months later in Milan, at La Scala, where it was conducted by Arturo Toscanini with Giuseppe Borgatti as Cavaradossi and the other principals as at Rome. The first foreign performance was given at Buenos Aires in June the same year, followed on 12 July by the London première, at Covent Garden, with Milka Ternina as Tosca ('a true creation' according to Puccini), Fernando de Lucia as Cavaradossi and Antonio Scotti as Scarpia (a role in which he specialized until the end of his career 33 years later). He and Ternina appeared in the New York première (4 February 1901), together with Giuseppe Cremonini (Puccini's first Des Grieux) as Cavaradossi. Since then outstanding Toscas have included Geraldine Farrar, Maria Jeritza (who sang 'Vissi d'arte' lying prone), Maria Caniglia and, later, Maria Callas, whose performances with Tito Gobbi as Scarpia became legendary.

*

ACT 1 *Interior of the church of San Andrea della Valle* The
curtain rises to a progression of three very loud, heavy chords, the
last producing a violent tonal wrench (ex.1, a motif that will connote
the villainous police chief Scarpia throughout the opera). The fugitive Angelotti hurries into the church, searches frantically for a key
concealed in a shrine of the Madonna and slips into the private chapel
of the Attavanti family. The Sacristan enters to a characteristic *buffo*
motif. He carries a bundle of paintbrushes which he proceeds grum-
blingly to wash. They belong to Cavaradossi, who arrives to put the
finishing touches to his portrait of the Magdalen. He contemplates
his canvas, in which he has succeeded in blending the dusky, southern
charms of his beloved Tosca with the blonde beauty of an unknown
woman whom he has often observed at prayer in the church
('Recondita armonia'). The aria is punctuated by asides from the
Sacristan. The Sacristan leaves, whereupon Angelotti emerges from
hiding; he is recognized by a shocked Cavaradossi, who hastily locks
the church door. Angelotti explains that he has just escaped from the
Castel Sant'Angelo, where he had been imprisoned by order of
Scarpia.

Their conversation is interrupted by the sound of Tosca's voice
outside the church. Angelotti again retreats into the chapel, while
Cavaradossi admits the singer, who enters in a mood of jealous suspi-
cion – she is sure she heard voices – though her accompanying music
conveys a dignified and beautiful presence. Reassured with some
difficulty by Cavaradossi, she suggests that they should go to his villa
in the country after her evening performance. Cavaradossi, his mind
on Angelotti, responds absently. Tosca is further disturbed by the
painting, with its resemblance to someone other than herself –

the Marchesa Attavanti. For the moment she accepts the painter's explanation and joins him in a tender love duet whose principal theme, occurring at the words 'Mia gelosa', functions as the motif for their mutual passion. Their conversation is not set as a conventional duet until, at the words 'Qual' occhio al mondo', a typically long-arched Puccini melody leads to a brief unison passage (four bars), but dissolves once more into conversation as Tosca leaves, to a delicate wind and harp accompaniment.

Cavaradossi and Angelotti plot the latter's escape. After dark he must make for Cavaradossi's villa in female disguise and in the event of danger hide in a well in the garden. A cannon shot from the Castel Sant'Angelo warns that Angelotti's flight has been discovered. At the same time the Sacristan re-enters with the news (false, as it turns out) of Napoleon's defeat at Marengo. The church fills with a joyous throng. At the height of the tumult Scarpia himself appears with Spoletta and other police agents. He rebukes the crowd for desecrating the atmosphere of a church and orders the Sacristan to make ready for a *Te Deum* in honour of the victory. Meanwhile he orders his men to look for clues to Angelotti's presence, which are soon found: a key, a basket empty of provisions which Cavaradossi, the Sacristan tells him, had left untouched; and a fan belonging to the Marchesa Attavanti, Angelotti's sister. When Tosca returns, Scarpia uses the fan to arouse her jealousy, always easily excited. To a recollection of the love-duet she hurries away in tears to the villa to surprise, as she thinks, the guilty pair. Scarpia gives orders for her to be followed, and in a monologue, over a characteristically obsessive pattern of alternating chords, accompanied by bells, organ, drum-beats to simulate cannon-fire and again the growling bassoons, gloats at the prospect of capturing the fugitive and enjoying the prima donna's favours; as the *Te Deum* swells to a climax he exclaims, 'Tosca, you make me forget God!'.

ACT 2 *Scarpia's apartment in the Palazzo Farnese* Scarpia is dining alone, while below at an entertainment given by Queen Caroline a gavotte is being danced. Spoletta enters to report on his fruitless search of Cavaradossi's villa for traces of Angelotti.

Scarpia's fury is mollified when he hears that his men have arrested Cavaradossi himself and brought him to the palace. During the singing of a cantata in the Queen's honour, led by Tosca, Scarpia interrogates the painter in the presence of the executioner, Roberti, and a judge of the criminal court. The choir, with Tosca's voice rising above it, provides an occasionally dissonant, tense background to Scarpia's opening interrogation, accompanied only by low strings and woodwind. As the cantata finishes Scarpia becomes more insistent, then, at Tosca's entrance, sings, 'con forza e sostenuto', 'Mario Cavaradossi, the Judge awaits your testimony'. Cavaradossi denies all knowledge of Angelotti, at which Scarpia gives orders for him to be tortured in an adjoining room. Tosca also refuses to reveal Angelotti's whereabouts (her words 'Non so nulla' are echoed by the strings), until, overcome by Cavaradossi's groans she mentions the well in the garden. Scarpia suspends the torture. Apprised of her betrayal Cavaradossi curses her for her weakness. Sciarrone comes in with the news that the Battle of Marengo had in fact been won by Napoleon.

Cavaradossi breaks out in a paean to liberty, for which Scarpia has him again put under arrest and marched to prison to be shot at dawn. He then promises to have the painter set free on condition that Tosca yield to his embraces. This prompts from Tosca the aria 'Vissi d'arte', into which Puccini weaves the motif that accompanied her first appearance. Spoletta enters and announces that Angelotti has killed himself. Scarpia turns to Tosca and she accepts his terms; he then bids Spoletta set up a mock-execution 'as in the case of Palmieri'. Tosca insists that he write her and Cavaradossi a safe-conduct. While he does so she catches sight of a knife lying to hand. A sinister motif on the strings indicates the thought going through her mind. No sooner has Scarpia finished writing than she stabs him and as he expires the 'knife' theme is played on full strings. Before leaving with the safe-conduct she places candles at his head and feet and a crucifix on his breast in conformity with her religious upbringing, and sings on a repeated middle C (although the words are often spoken instead) 'E avanti a lui tremava tutta Roma!' ('And before him all Rome trembled!').

ACT 3   *A platform in the Castel Sant'Angelo*   A prelude evokes the breaking of dawn. A Shepherd-boy is heard singing as he drives his flock. The sound of sheep-bells gives way to the mingled chimes of matins. Cavaradossi enters accompanied by the melody of the aria he will sing, heard here for the first time, 'con molta anima', on the strings. To a reminiscence of the Act 1 love-duet played on solo cellos Cavaradossi asks for pen and paper with which to write a farewell letter to Tosca. His anguish at leaving her for ever is expressed in the aria 'E lucevan le stelle', a recollection of past bliss before the final darkness, with a mournful clarinet taking the main line before he sings it at the words 'O dolci baci, languide carezze'. Spoletta arrives with Tosca, then retires. Tosca produces the safe-conduct and explains to a suspicious Cavaradossi how she obtained it and how she repaid the giver. Cavaradossi is astonished and delighted. Their tender exchanges are continually overshadowed by Tosca's concern for her lover – will he be able to act his part convincingly during the mock-execution? But when the firing squad arrives he plays his part all too well, for the rifles are loaded, and Tosca finds herself addressing his lifeless body. Meanwhile the news of Scarpia's murder has broken. Spoletta, Sciarrone and the other agents are heard calling for Tosca's blood. She climbs on to the battlements and, crying that she and Scarpia will meet before God, Tosca leaps to her death, to an orchestral peroration of Cavaradossi's 'E lucevan le stelle'.

*

None of Puccini's operas has aroused more hostility than *Tosca*, by reason of its alleged coarseness and brutality, (the musicologist Joseph Kerman referred to it, notoriously, as a 'shabby little schocker'); yet its position in the central repertory has remained unchallenged. Not only is it theatrically gripping from start to finish: it presents the composer's most varied and interesting soprano role, hence its perennial appeal for the great operatic actress. In contrast to Sardou's heroine, against whose ignorance and simplicity the playwright can never resist tilting, Puccini's Tosca is a credible woman of the theatre, lacking neither intelligence nor humour, and capable of genuine dignity. Nowhere is she more moving than in Act 3, in which she imagines herself to be in command of the situation and that all she has to do is to teach Cavaradossi how to act. All the more heart-rending is her discovery of the truth.

Tosca is the most Wagnerian of Puccini's scores in its use of motifs, every one of which refers to a single object, person or idea, though none of them is developed or modified. But, like Wagner, he sometimes used them to give us information about a character's unexpressed thoughts. An instance of this occurs in Act 1 where Tosca asks Cavaradossi to meet her that evening. 'This evening?', he queries in alarm, and the orchestra plays a snatch of the motif associated with Angelotti. Likewise Scarpia's interrogation of the painter is punctuated by a motif connoting the well, which Cavaradossi refuses to mention, but of which he is obviously thinking. The only weakness in the drama is Puccini's inept handling of the political element; but issues of this kind held no interest for the composer of *La bohème*, *Tosca* and *Madama Butterfly*.

J.B.

Madama Butterfly
('Madam Butterfly')

Tragedia giapponese in two acts set to a libretto by Giuseppe Giacosa and Luigi Illica after David Belasco's play *Madame Butterfly*, itself based on John Luther Long's short story, which in turn was based partly on Pierre Loti's tale *Madame Chrysanthème*. *Madama Butterfly* was first performed in Milan at the Teatro alla Scala, on 17 February 1904; the revised version was first performed in Brescia, at the Teatro Grande, on 28 May 1904; the definitive version, though in French, was first performed at the Opéra Comique, on 28 December 1906.

The cast at the première included Rosina Storchio (Butterfly), Giovanni Zenatello (Pinkerton) and Giuseppe de Luca Sharpless). The conductor was Cleofante Campanini.

Cio-Cio-San [Madam Butterfly]	soprano
Suzuki	mezzo-soprano
F. B. Pinkerton *Lieutenant in the United States Army*	tenor
Sharpless *United States consul at Nagasaki*	baritone
Goro *a marriage broker*	tenor
Prince Yamadori	tenor
The Bonze ⎫ *Cio-Cio-San's uncles*	bass
Yakuside ⎭	bass
The Imperial Commissioner	bass
The Official Registrar	bass
Cio-Cio-San's mother	mezzo-soprano
The Aunt	soprano
The Cousin	soprano
Kate Pinkerton	mezzo-soprano
Dolore ('Trouble') *Cio-Cio-San's child*	silent

Cio-Cio-San's relations and friends and Servants

Setting Nagasaki, the beginning of the 20th century

Puccini was seized with the subject after seeing Belasco's play performed in London in June 1900, and he immediately applied to Belasco for the rights. These, however, were not officially granted until September of the following year. In the meantime Puccini had sent a copy of Long's story to Illica, who drew up a scheme in two parts. The first, originally intended as a prologue, derived exclusively from Long (with comic embellishments in the spirit of Loti) and showed the wedding of Pinkerton and Cio-Cio-San (called Butterfly by her friends); the second covered the action of Belasco's play and was divided into three scenes, the first and last being set in Butterfly's house and the second in the American consulate. As Giacosa proceeded with the versification the prologue expanded into Act 1 and the first scene of the second part into Act 2, while Illica's intention of retaining Long's ending (with Butterfly's suicide interrupted by the arrival of her child and the maid Suzuki who bandaged her wounds) was overruled in favour of Belasco's final catastrophe. Not until November 1902 was the libretto complete, whereupon Puccini decided in spite of strenuous opposition from Giacosa to abolish the scene in the American consulate, and with it the contrast between a Japanese and a Western ambience desired by Illica. Instead the two remaining scenes of the second part were to be fused into a single act lasting an hour and a half. So convinced was Giacosa of the folly of this arrangement that he wanted the text of the missing scene to be printed in the libretto; but Ricordi refused.

The composition was interrupted in February 1903 by a motor accident from which Puccini made a long and painful convalescence. The score was completed by December and the première fixed for February the following year with an outstanding cast. Although the singers and orchestra showed much enthusiasm, the first night was a disaster; the opera was subjected to what Puccini described as 'a veritable lynching'. That the audience's hostility was deliberately engineered has never been doubted; all the evidence points to Ricordi's chief rival, Sonzogno, as the prime mover. Puccini was accused of plagiarism of himself and other composers. He at once withdrew the opera, and although convinced of its merits he made alterations to the score before allowing it to be performed elsewhere.

He discarded several details involving Butterfly's relations in Act 1, divided the long second act into two parts separated by an interval and added the arietta 'Addio, fiorito asil' for Pinkerton. The second performance took place on 28 May that same year at the Teatro Grande, Brescia, Salomea Krusceniski replacing Rosina Storchio among the original cast. This time the opera enjoyed a triumph.

Nonetheless further modifications were to follow, mainly affecting Act 1. These ended with the Paris première, which was given by the Opéra-Comique on 28 December 1906, and formed the basis of the definitive printed edition. At the suggestion of Albert Carré, the theatre director and husband of the prima donna Marguerite, Puccini further softened Pinkerton's character, eliminating his more xeno-phobic utterances, and avoided the confrontation between Butterfly and Kate, who thus emerges as a more sympathetic character. Earlier that year, however, Ricordi had already brought out a vocal score in which many of the original passages can be found. Three of them, all from Act 1 were reinstated with Puccini's sanction for a revival at the Teatro Carcano, Milan, shortly after World War I (they were not, however, reprinted). Joachim Herz's production of *Madama Butterfly* in 1978 restored some of the original music from the auto-graph, and the earliest version was given complete at La Fenice in 1982 and at Leeds in 1991. Outstanding exponents of the title role have included Geraldine Farrar, Toti dal Monte (Toscanini's favourite interpreter), Victoria de los Angeles, Elizabeth Vaughan (in English), and later Renata Scotto and Mirella Freni, as well as several Japanese singers.

*

ACT 1 *A hill near Nagasaki; in the foreground a Japanese house with terrace and garden* An orchestral fugato sets a scene of bustling activity as Goro leads Lieutenant Pinkerton out of the house, demon-strating its various appurtenances, in particular the sliding panels – so ridiculously fragile, the lieutenant thinks. The domestic staff are pre-sented to him: a cook, a servant and his future wife's maid, Suzuki, who at once begins to bore Pinkerton with her chatter. While Goro is reeling off the list of wedding guests, Sharpless enters out of breath, having climbed the hill from Nagasaki. A characteristic motif establishes his benign, good-humoured presence. At Goro's bidding servants bring drinks and wicker chairs for Sharpless and his host. Pinkerton explains that he has bought the house on a 999-year lease which may be terminated at a month's notice. In his solo 'Dovunque al mondo', framed by the opening strain of *The Star-Spangled Banner* (later used as a recurrent motif), Pinkerton outlines his philosophy – that of the roving 'Yankee' who takes his pleasure where he finds it ('an easy-going gospel', observes Sharpless). After sending Goro to fetch the bride, Pinkerton dilates on her charms and his own infatuation. Sharpless recollects having heard her voice when she paid a visit to the consulate. Its ring of simple sincerity touched him deeply and he hopes that Pinkerton will never hurt her. Pinkerton scoffs at his scruples, so typical of unadventurous middle age. Both drink a toast to America (*The Star-Spangled Banner* again) and, in Pinkerton's case, to the day when he will take home an American wife.

Goro announces the arrival of Butterfly and her friends, heralded by the distant sound of humming female voices. As the procession draws nearer the orchestra unfolds a radiant theme that begins with a series of rising sequences, each phrase ending on a whole-tone chord, then evolves into an extended periodic melody to which an essentially pentatonic motif of Japanese origin (ex.1) forms a hushed coda. Butterfly whose voice has been heard soaring above those of the female throng, has by now appeared. She bows to the two men. Sharpless questions her about her family and background. He learns that her people were once wealthy but have since fallen on hard times, so that she has been forced to earn her living as a geisha. She is 15 years old. Sharpless repeats his warning to Pinkerton. More guests arrive, including Butterfly's mother, a Cousin, an Aunt and Uncle Yakuside, who immediately asks for wine. Meanwhile the women exchange impressions of the bridegroom (not all of them favourable) until at a sign from Butterfly they all kowtow to Pinkerton and disperse. Butterfly shows Pinkerton her treasures and mementos, which she keeps concealed in her voluminous sleeves – a clasp a clay pipe, a girdle, a pot of rouge (which she throws away in response to Pinkerton's mocking glance) and a narrow sheath which she hurriedly carries into the house. Goro explains that it holds the dagger with which Butterfly's father killed himself by the emperor's command. Re-emerging, she produces puppets that represent the spirits of her forebears. But she adds that she has recently visited the American mission to renounce her ancestral religion and embrace that of her husband (ex. 1 returns). Goro calls for silence; the Imperial Commissioner proclaims the wedding and all join in a toast to the couple's happiness, 'O Kami! O Kami!'. (At this point in the original version there was a drunken arietta for Yakuside who broke off to chastise a badly behaved child.) The festivities are interrupted by the Bonze, who bursts in denouncing Butterfly for having forsworn her faith. As her relations scatter in horror the orchestra embodies their curse in a whole-tone motif. Alone with his bride Pinkerton comforts her, while Suzuki can be heard muttering her evening prayers to the gods of Japan. There follows an extended duet for the lovers ('Viene la sera') woven from several melodic threads, now rapturous, now tender and delicate. Twice the 'curse' motif intrudes, first as Butterfly recalls how her family has cast her off, then when she remembers how the most beautiful butterflies are often impaled with a pin. The duet concludes with a grandiose reprise of the theme which accompanied her first appearance.

Ex.1

ACT 2 Part i *Inside Butterfly's house*   Three years have gone by. Butterfly is alone with Suzuki, who is praying to the Japanese gods that her mistress's sufferings may soon end. Butterfly retorts that such gods are lazy; Pinkerton's God would soon come to her aid if only

He knew where to find her. Their funds are nearly exhausted and Suzuki doubts whether Pinkerton will ever return. Furious, Butterfly reminds her how he had arranged for the consul to pay the rent, how he had put locks on the doors, and how he had promised to return 'when the robins build their nests'. In a celebrated aria ('Un bel dì vedremo') she pictures the scene of Pinkerton's return and her own joy. Goro arrives with Sharpless, who brings a letter from the lieutenant. Butterfly gives him a cordial welcome, and asks him how often the robins build their nests in America. Sharpless is evasive.

Prince Yamadori enters and makes Butterfly an offer of marriage, which she mockingly rejects: she is a married woman according to the laws of America, where divorce, she says is a punishable offense. Yamadori leaves and Sharpless begins to read the letter, breaking the news that Pinkerton intends to go out of Butterfly's life for ever, but she misunderstands the letter's drift and he abandons the task. He asks what she would do if Pinkerton were never to return, and she replies that she could resume her profession as a geisha, but that she would rather die by her own hand. Sharpless angers her by advising her to accept Yamadori's offer, but then she hurries to fetch her son by Pinkerton; astonished and moved, Sharpless promises to inform the father and leaves. Suzuki drags in Goro, whom she has caught spreading slanderous rumours about the child's parentage. Butterfly threatens to kill him, then dismisses him with contempt. The harbour cannon signals the arrival of a ship. To an orchestral reprise of 'Un bel dì' Butterfly seizes a telescope and makes out the name *Abraham Lincoln* – Pinkerton's man-of-war. She and Suzuki proceed to deck the house with blossom in a duet ('Scuoti quella fronda di ciliegio'). After adorning herself 'as on our wedding day' she, Suzuki and the child settle to a night of waiting, while an unseen chorus of wordless voices recalling the theme to which Sharpless attempted to read Pinkerton's letter, evokes the slowly fading light.

ACT 2 Part ii   An interlude, originally joined to the previous humming chorus, depicts Butterfly's restless thoughts; then, to the distant cries of the sailors the sun rises to disclose Butterfly, Suzuki and the child seated as before. Butterfly sings a lullaby and takes the boy to another room, where she quickly falls asleep. Pinkerton appears with Sharpless. Suzuki catches sight of a woman in the garden and Sharpless tells her that it is Pinkerton's wife, Kate. Their concern, he tells her, is to ensure the child a good American upbringing. He reproaches the lieutenant for his heartlessness. Pinkerton pours out his grief and remorse in the *romanza* that Puccini added for Brescia ('Addio, fiorito asil') and leaves, unable to face the bride he has betrayed. Butterfly enters, to confront Sharpless, Suzuki and Kate. When the situation is explained to her she reacts with good dignity; she bids them retire and return in half an hour. She takes a last farewell of her child and stabs herself behind a screen with her father's dagger. Pinkerton is heard desperately calling her name.

*

No Puccini opera testifies more strongly than *Madama Butterfly* to his ability to discern the possibilities for music drama in a trivial play performed in a language of which he hardly understood a word. Here he and his librettists (working as always under his own direction) fleshed out Belasco's pathetic but ridiculous puppet into a genuine figure of tragedy who proceeds during the action from child-like innocence to an adult understanding and a calm acceptance of the destiny which her code of honour enjoins upon her. Butterfly is the apotheosis of the frail suffering heroine so often encountered in Puccini's gallery; and he would return to her only once more in the slave-girl Liù in *Turandot*.

By making use of at least seven Japanese folk melodies the composer both evoked the Far Eastern ambience and enlarged his musical vocabulary, since every one of them is assimilated into his own personal and by now highly sophisticated style. The scale of musical thought is likewise grander than ever before, the love duet in Act 1 being the longest and most elaborate that Puccini ever wrote. Though the organization remains for the most part motivic the motifs are no longer always referential in the Wagnerian manner. The whole-tone curse motif, is not always associated with the Bonze, while ex.1 receives its fullest treatment where Butterfly tells Pinkerton about her visit to the American mission in order to embrace her husband's religion ('Io seguo il mio destino') – an event that has no bearing on the theme's first appearance. In his later operas Puccini tended more and more to use motifs without hard and fast associations.

J.B.

La fanciulla del West

('The Girl of the West' [*The Girl of the Golden West*])

Opera in three acts set to a libretto by Guelfo Civinini and Carlo Zangarini after David Belasco's play *The Girl of the Golden West*; first performed in New York at the Metropolitan Opera House, on 10 December 1910.

The cast at the première included Emmy Destinn (Minnie), Enrico Caruso (Dick Johnson) and Pasquale Amato (Jack Rance), with Antonio Pini-Corsi, creator of Schaunard in *La bohème*, in the minute role of Happy. The conductor was Toscanini.

Minnie	soprano
Jack Rance *sheriff*	baritone
Dick Johnson/Ramerrez *bandit*	tenor
Nick *bartender at the Polka saloon*	tenor
Ashby *Well's Fargo agent*	bass
Sonora	baritone
Trin	tenor
Sid	baritone
Bello	baritone
Harry *miners*	tenor
Joe	tenor
Happy	baritone
Larkens	bass
Billy Jackrabbit *a Red Indian*	bass
Wowkle *his squaw*	mezzo-soprano
Jake Wallace *a travelling camp minstral*	baritone
José Castro (*mestizo*) *one of Ramerrez's band*	bass
The Pony Express Rider	tenor

Men of the camp and boys of the ridge

Setting A miners' camp at the foot of the Cloudy Mountains, California, during the gold rush, 1849–50

Early in 1907, during his first visit to New York for the Metropolitan premières of *Manon Lescaut* and *Madama Butterfly*, Puccini saw three of Belasco's plays performed on Broadway, among them *The Girl of the Golden West*. He was not enthusiastic. 'I like the ambience of the West', he wrote to Tito Ricordi (son of Giulio), 'but in all the "pièces" I've seen I've found only a few scenes here and there. Never a simple thread, all muddle and at times bad taste and old hat'. However, a seed had been sown; and when at the end of May Puccini went to London, his friend Sybil Seligman urged him to consider Belasco's drama, an Italian translation of which she procured for him.

By July Puccini was firmly decided. He wrote to his publisher asking him to obtain the rights as well as the author's permission to make certain changes to the action (these would amount to transferring the 'schoolmarm' episode from the third act to the first and writing an new final act set in the Californian forest, the action of which derives mostly from Octave Mirbeau's play *Les mauvais bergers*, a subject which Puccini had proposed in 1905, but which Luigi Illica had vetoed as too left-wing).

Of his previous librettists, Giuseppe Giacosa had died and Illica was fully engaged on a libretto about Marie Antoinette (for which Puccini had contracted but which he never set). Tito Ricordi indicated Carlo Zangarini as the ideal collaborator, especially since his mother was American. In August the contracts were signed for what Puccini foretold would prove 'a second *Bohème*, only stronger, bolder and more spacious'.

Zangarini completed the libretto in January 1908. Puccini was satisfied with his general scheme but insisted that he take on a partner to polish the details. Zangarini threatened to go to law, but eventually agreed to collaborate with the Livornese poet Guelfo Civinini. By May the first two acts had been reworked to Puccini's satisfaction and he was able to begin composition, but in October a domestic tragedy occurred which caused a hiatus of nine months. Resuming in August 1909, Puccini completed the score a year later. To Sybil Seligman goes the credit for settling on the exact title. The opera was dedicated to the British queen, Alexandra, a keen admirer of Puccini's music, which often figured in private concerts at Buckingham Palace organized by Sir Paolo Tosti, music master to the royal family and himself a close friend of the composer.

In November 1910 Puccini set sail for America for what would be the first world première ever held at the Metropolitan. No expense had been spared. Belasco himself assisted Tito Ricordi with the production. To all appearances the opera was a triumphant success, the composer receiving 55 curtain calls, but the critics were guarded. The Covent Garden première followed on 29 May 1911, again in Puccini's presence, conducted by Cleofonte Campanini with Emmy Destinn (Minnie), Amadeo Bassi (Johnson) and the Metropolitan's Sonora, Dinh Gilly as Jack Rance. There the reception was less encouraging. *La fanciulla del West* was finally introduced to Italy at the Teatro Costanzi, Rome, on 12 June that year under Toscanini, with Eugenia Burzio (Minnie), Amadeo Bassi (Johnson) and Pasquale Amato (Rance), but it achieved no more than a *succès d'estime*. Although Puccini declared it his best opera to date it failed to enter the general repertory; nor until late in the century was it estimated at its true worth. However, the tenor solo from Act 3, 'Ch'ella mi creda libero e lontano', is said to have been sung by Italian troops during World War I as an equivalent to the English song 'It's a long way to Tipperary'.

ACT 1 *The Polka saloon, at sunset* A prelude, intended by Puccini to evoke the vast Californian forest, presents two important ideas: the lyrical theme associated with the hero and heroine's first embrace (ex.1) and a modified version of the cake-walk motif which on its later appearance connotes the bandit Ramerrez. Then the distant voices of the approaching miners are heard. They enter in twos and threes to a hoedown theme, to be welcomed by Nick. Happy, Harry, Bello and Joe sit down to a game of faro with Sid as banker. Jake Wallace regales the company with the nostalgic song 'Che faranno i vecchi miei' (ex.2, one of the most frequently repeated motifs in the opera), which causes Larkens to break down in tears. All present contribute money for his passage home. Sid is caught cheating and the miners threaten to hang him, but Rance pins a two of spades to his lapel as a mark of shame and has him thrown out of the saloon. Ashby arrives with news of the imminent capture of the bandit

Ramerrez. A quarrel breaks out between Rance and Sonora, both in love with Minnie, and Sonora draws a revolver. Trin grabs his arm and diverts the shot. The appearance of Minnie herself to a broad, wide-intervalled theme (ex.3, a fine example of Puccini's newly enriched harmonic style) calms the atmosphere. The miners offer her their modest gifts and settle down to a bible-class, which she takes.

Ex.1 Allegro non troppo

Ex.2 JAKE WALLACE
Andante tranquillo

Che fa – ran-noi vec-chi miei là lon – ta – no, là lon-

– ta – no? che fa – ran – no

['What will my old folks be doing there, far away?']

Ex.3 Andante vibrato

The Pony Express Rider arrives with the mail and Ashby interrogates him about one Nina Micheltorena, the bandit's mistress, who is expected to reveal his whereabouts. The men go into the adjoining dance hall leaving Rance alone with Minnie. He declares his love for her and talks of his unhappy background ('Minnie, dalla mia casa'). She, knowing him to be already married, imagines a different picture of domestic bliss based on memories of her own happy childhood ('Laggiù nel Soledad, ero piccina'). Nick returns with a stranger, whose identity is betrayed to the audience by the 'Ramerrez' motif. He gives his name as Johnson. Rance takes an instant dislike to him and orders the men to force him to account for his presence. But Minnie, who remembers once meeting him on the road, vouches for him. A waltz is struck up in the hall, where Minnie and Johnson dance together. Ashby and a group of men enter from outside dragging in José Castro. Pretending to have deserted Ramerrez's band, Castro promises to lead them to the chief. His real purpose is to draw the miners away from the Polka so that Ramerrez may rob the saloon. When Johnson re-enters Castro manages to whisper to him his plan – a whistle outside will be the signal for him to proceed. The miners prepare to ride away with Castro, leaving Minnie to guard their earnings. She and Johnson express their dawning sympathy for one another in a duet based mainly on a reprise of the waltz melody. The whistle is heard but Johnson takes no action. He accepts Minnie's invitation to visit her later at her mountain hut, then leaves. Nick returns to find Minnie absorbed in the recollection of Johnson's last words to her – that she has the face of an angel. To echoes of ex.3 the curtain falls.

ACT 2 *Minnie's cabin, later that evening* Wowkle sings to her child a lullaby that develops into a duet with Billy Jackrabbit as both think vaguely of getting married. Minnie enters, orders supper for two and with subdued excitement prepares to receive her visitor. Johnson arrives; Minnie fends off his attempt to embrace her and to a recall of the waltz they begin a decorous conversation, during which Minnie describes her life at the camp ('Oh, se sapeste'). As Wowkle brings the food the orchestra outlines a pentatonic theme loosely related to the waltz that will frame the love duet, whose central movement is evolved from ex.1, initially twisted into a whole-tone scale. Johnson offers to leave, but a blizzard makes it necessary for him to stay the night.

The posse headed by Rance knock at the door. After concealing Johnson behind the bed-curtain Minnie admits them. They are concerned for her safety, Rance tells her, having discovered that Johnson is in fact Ramerrez and is still in the neighbourhood. Minnie sends them away, then rounds angrily on her guest. Remorsefully he makes excuses for his past life, which he now intends to abandon for ever. Minnie can forgive the bandit, but not the man who stole her first kiss under false pretences, and she orders him out of the house. A shot rings out, and he staggers back against the door wounded. Minnie helps him into the attic before Rance arrives, certain that he has found his man. Minnie defies him to search the premises. Thwarted, Rance is about to leave when a drop of blood falls from the ceiling onto his hand. Ignoring Minnie's protests he orders Johnson to come down. Johnson does so and collapses in a faint. Minnie plays her last card. Knowing Rance to be a gambler she challenges him to a game of poker. If he wins, he may take her as his 'wife'; if he loses then Johnson belongs to her. Rance accepts, and is on the point of winning when she pretends to feel faint; as he goes to fetch her a glass of water she takes a new pack of cards from her stocking and lays out a winning hand. He accepts her victory with bad grace.

ACT 3   *A clearing in the Californian forest at dawn, some time later*
Rance and Nick are brooding before a fire; Ashby, Billy Jackrabbit and several miners are sleeping nearby. Nick attempts to console Rance, commending his gallant behaviour in dealing with Minnie. At the sound of distant voices Ashby and the men wake up and joyfully predict the bandit's capture. Rance exults in the prospect of revenge, while Ashby hurries away to join the man-hunt. As the orchestra builds up an impressive action scene recalling previous themes, various miners posted on the look-out describe Johnson's attempts to elude his pursuers. He is brought in tethered to his horse to face an accusing mob. Billy Jackrabbit is ordered to prepare a noose for the lynching, but is secretly bribed by Nick to take his time. Johnson proudly defends himself against the charge of murder. In the few minutes remaining to him he asks only that Minnie never be told of his fate. In the aria 'Ch'ella mi creda libero e lontano', the one self-contained piece in the entire score, he expresses the wish that she may believe him to have gone free to lead a better life in some distant land. Enraged, Rance punches him in the face; but Johnson's words have already caused the men to hesitate. Minnie rides in on horseback to a harmonically distorted version of ex.3.

When her pleas for mercy prove vain she rushes to Johnson's side, draws a pistol and threatens to shoot both him and herself. During the ensemble that follows opinion among the miners is divided. In the end it is Sonora who sways the balance. Johnson is released, and as he and Minnie ride away to a future of happiness the men bid their beloved 'sister' a sorrowful farewell to the strains of ex.2.

*

La fanciulla del West is a remarkable instance of self-renewal on the part of a composer who would seem to have exhausted a vein of predominantly feminine softness. The opera's atmosphere is unyieldingly masculine, at times brutal, the harmonies more astringent than ever before with plentiful use of whole-tone chords and unresolved dissonances, the rhythms vigorous, sometimes syncopated and the lyrical moments comparatively few. The influence of Debussy and the Richard Strauss of *Salome* is clear, though, as always, perfectly integrated within the composer's personal style. The Californian ambience is evoked with the aid of American folktunes and folk-dances, either authentic or imitated, with a Red Indian chant to characterize Billy Jackrabbit and his squaw. Minnie is unique among Puccini's heroines – cheerfully authoritative with a touch of the Puritan schoolmarm yet susceptible to tender passion and ready to compromise her strict principles in order to save the life of the man she loves.

Orchestrally *La fanciulla del West* is Puccini's most ambitious undertaking before *Turandot*, his forces including quadruple woodwind, two harps and an assortment of percussion, from all of which he distilled a vast range of instrumental colour from the delicate to the barbaric. Though it has never attained the easy popularity of its three predecessors, the opera has always won the respect of musicians, among them Weber and Ravel.

J.B.

La rondine
('The Swallow')

Commedia lirica in three acts set to a text by Giuseppe Adami after a libretto by A. M. Willner and Heinz Reichert; first performed in Monte Carlo, at the Théâtre de l'Opéra, on 27 March 1917.

The original cast included Gilda dalla Rizza (Magda), Ina Maria Ferraris (Lisette), Tito Schipa (Ruggero), Francesco Dominici (Prunier) and Gustave Huberdeau (Rambaldo); the conductor was Gino Marinuzzi.

Magda de Civry	soprano
Lisette *her maid*	soprano
Ruggero Lastouc	tenor
Prunier *a poet*	tenor
Rambaldo Fernandez *Magda's protector*	baritone
Périchaud	baritone/bass
Gobin	tenor
Crébillon	bass/baritone
Rabonnier	baritone
Yvette	soprano
Bianca	soprano
Suzy	mezzo-soprano
A Butler	bass
A Voice	soprano

Members of the bourgeoisie, students, painters, elegantly dressed ladies and gentlemen, *grisettes*, flower-girls and dancing girls, waiters

Setting Paris and the Riviera during the Second Empire

During a visit to Vienna in October 1913 for a performance of *La fanciulla del West* Puccini was invited by the directors of the Carltheater to compose an operetta. He agreed in principle, insisting, however, that it take the form of a through-composed comic opera 'like *Rosenkavalier* but more amusing and more organic'. Of two subjects offered successively by Willner and Reichert, Puccini chose the second and entrusted Adami with drawing up the Italian text. Work proceeded slowly over the next two years. In the meantime Italy's entry into World War I necessitated a revision of the contract, whereby the Viennese management resigned their claim to the opera's première while retaining what amounted to half the performing rights. Giulio Ricordi, Puccini's great champion, had died in 1912, and as his son, the younger Tito, showed no interest in the project Puccini contracted with the firm of Lorenzo Sonzogno for the publication. Because of the state of European hostilities it was decided to launch the opera on what was technically neutral territory; hence the choice of Monte Carlo. The first Italian performance took place at Bologna on 5 June the same year. During 1918–19 Puccini made various modifications to the score, allocating Prunier to a baritone, raising the pitch of Lisette's role here and there and adding a *romanza* in Act 1 for Ruggero ('Parigi è la città dei desideri'). In Act 2 he reduced the ensemble 'Bevo al tuo fresco sorriso' (based on a lullaby submitted to a periodical in 1912) to a quartet. In Act 3 he eliminated the quarrel between Prunier and Lisette while retaining much of the music, and assigned the final duet to Prunier and Magda. In this form the opera was given in Vienna (9 October 1920) at the Volksoper, where it met with little success. Later, Puccini prepared yet a third version in which the first two acts reverted to their original design, with Prunier once more a tenor. Act 3, however, was altered even more radically than before, introducing a trio of *vendeuses* whose wares Magda cannot afford to buy, restoring the quarrel between Prunier and Lisette and bringing in Rambaldo, to new music, with a purse of gold for his former mistress. Meanwhile Ruggero, informed of Magda's past by an anonymous letter, drives her away, where previously he had pleaded with her to stay. Magda would be on stage 'alone and abandoned' as the curtain fell. There is no record of this version's having been performed, nor is there any trace of the material, which was destroyed by bombing in World War II. All subsequent imprints of the score correspond with the original of 1917.

La rondine did not reach the Metropolitan, New York, until four years after the composer's death. It has never been seen at Covent Garden.

*

ACT 1 *An elegant salon in Magda's Parisian house* Prunier is holding forth to his hostess and her guests about the latest fashion for sentimental love. Lisette mocks the idea and is promptly sent about her business. Yet no one except Magda takes the poet very seriously. Prunier illustrates his theory with the story of his latest heroine, Doretta, who spurned a king's ransom for love ('Chi il bel sogno di Doretta potè indovinar'). Taking up a second verse, Magda completes the story, telling how the girl lost her heart to a student; and she repeats the refrain to her own words 'Folle amore!' In every heart, Prunier maintains, there lurks the devil of romantic love.

Rambaldo claims that he knows how to exorcise it; and he gives Magda a pearl necklace. She passes it round, to general admiration, but a gentle waltz theme indicates that her thoughts are elsewhere. Rambaldo retires, having received permission to present to her the son of a childhood acquaintance. Meantime she regales her friends with her account of an innocent flirtation with a student at Bullier's Restaurant ('Ore dolci e divine'), to which his words 'Fanciulla, è sbocciato l'amore' form a waltz-like refrain. Rambaldo returns with the visitor, Ruggero Lestouc, as Magda is having her palm read by Prunier, who predicts that, like the swallow of the opera's title, she will fly south to love and happiness. The company are profuse with suggestions as to where Ruggero shall spend his first night out in Paris. The choice falls on Bullier's. As the guests leave Magda decides to remain at home, then thinks better of it and retires to her boudoir to change. Meanwhile Prunier flirts with Lisette to a sly, insinuating orchestral theme. As it is her evening off, they decide to dine out together, Lisette wearing one of her mistress's hats. When they have left Magda emerges dressed as a *grisette*, ready for an adventure at Bullier's, her mind full of Prunier's prophecy and 'Doretta's' secret.

ACT 2 *Chez Bullier* The restaurant is alive with a crowd of students, artists, flower-girls and *grisettes*. Ruggero is alone at a table.

Magda appears and to the importunities of the students she replies that she is meeting somebody; whereupon they lead her to Ruggero's table. The young man fails to recognize her, but they converse amicably. Magda teases him about his probable love-affairs; to which he replies that if he should fall in love it would be for ever. He persuades her to join him in a waltz, which grows in grandeur and vivacity, incorporating reminiscences from Act 1. Prunier arrives with Lisette. The dance concluded, Magda and Ruggero return to their table and pledge their newly born love, she giving her name as Paulette. Lisette starts at the sight of her mistress; but Prunier, at a sign from Magda, convinces the girl that it is only a chance resemblance. Both couples begin a slow concertato ('Bevo al tuo fresco sorriso'), which comes to a sudden halt as Rambaldo appears at the head of the stairs. Prunier tells Lisette to keep Ruggero out of sight. Rambaldo asks Magda for an explanation and she replies that she intends to leave him; he bows ironically and retires. Ruggero returns with Magda's shawl, and the two leave to begin a new life together.

Act 3   *The Côte d'Azur*   On the terrace of a pavilion overlooking the Mediterranean Magda and Ruggero are exchanging thoughts about their first meeting and present happiness. But their money is running out. Ruggero is not unduly worried; he says that he has written to his mother for her consent to their marriage and he paints an idyllic picture of his home in the country. Magda is horrified, for Ruggero knows nothing of her past as *demi-mondaine*. She goes into the pavilion as Prunier and Lisette arrive. The girl is in an uncontrollable state of nerves: Prunier had tried to make her a music-hall singer, but her début had been disastrous. Magda greets them and gladly agrees to take Lisette once more into service. Prunier delivers a message from Rambaldo: he is ready to welcome her back on any terms. As Lisette goes to resume her duties Prunier leaves, but not before asking to know her evenings off. Magda is joined by Ruggero, joyfully brandishing his mother's reply: she is delighted that her son has found a virtuous bride and looks forward to meeting her. Heartbroken, Magda reveals she is not a virtuous innocent and declares that she can never be Ruggero's wife. Their last, anguished duet ('Ma come puoi lasciarmi') takes the form of a cabaletta with orchestral peroration over a vocal 'parlante'; Ruggero collapses in tears, while Magda, supported by Lisette, makes her way slowly out of his life.

*

In its musical organization *La rondine* follows a characteristic Puccinian motivic pattern in which there is more room than usual for extended melodies, that are in turn often broken down into recurring motifs. Second Empire Paris is evoked by frequent waltz rhythms of the slower French rather than the Viennese variety; but there are also occasional hints of more modern dances such as the tango, one-step and even (in the lovers' duet in Act 2 'Perche mai cercate') the slow foxtrot. The large orchestral forces are delicately handled, and a number of harmonic audacities worthy of *La fanciulla del West* merely add piquancy to a score of unusual elegance. The main musical weight is thrown into Act 2, where two of the waltz themes are combined vertically, and whose concertato remains the lyrical pinnacle of the opera. In Act 3 the level of invention falls, probably because the theme of renunciation failed to fire Puccini's dramatic instinct. (That the act was written three times to a different plot but (mostly) to the same music tells its own story.) Hence, perhaps, the opera's virtual exclusion from the repertory.

J.B.

Il tabarro
('The Cloak')

Opera in one act set to a libretto by Giuseppe Adami after Didier Gold's play *La houppelande*; first performed in New York, at the Metropolitan Opera, on 14 December 1918 (as the first part of *Il trittico*).

The original cast included Claudia Muzio (Giorgetta), Alice Gentle (La Frugola), Giulio Crimi (Luigi), Luigi Montesanto (Michele), Angelo Bada (Tinca) and Adam Didur (Talpa); the conductor was Roberto Moranzoni.

Michele *a barge-owner (aged 50)*	Baritone
Giorgetta *Michele's wife (aged 25)*	Soprano
Luigi *a stevedore (aged 20)*	tenor
Il 'Tinca' ('tench') *a stevedore (aged 35)*	tenor
Il 'Talpa' ('mole') *a stevedore (aged 55)*	bass
La Frugola ('the rummage') *Talpa's wife (aged 50)*	mezzo-soprano

Stevedores, a ballad-seller, *midinettes*, an organ-grinder and two lovers

Setting A bank of the river Seine

Il tabarro is the first item in a triple bill of contrasted one-act operas, a project which Puccini had cherished for many years but from which he had been regularly dissuaded by Giulio Ricordi as being harmful to the box office. Not until Ricordi's death in 1912 did he feel free to proceed. The first subject was found easily enough: Didier Gold's play *La houppelande*, which Puccini saw performed at the Théâtre Marigny in Paris in autumn that year and which he described to Luigi Illica as '*apache* in every sense of the word, and almost, no, more than almost, *Grand Guignol*'. But relations with his old librettist had begun to turn sour; and it was to the young playwright Giovacchino Forzano that Puccini first turned for a suitable text. Forzano, however, was unwilling to adapt someone else's work (in due course he would furnish the other two panels of the 'triptych', *Suor Angelica* and *Gianni Schicchi*, from his own invention) and suggested instead the poet and diplomat Ferdinando Martini. When after a few months he too bowed out, having decided that the profession of librettist was not for him, Puccini approached Giuseppe Adami, who accepted with alacrity his first commission from the composer. Progress was held up for a time by their joint work on *La rondine*, the German text of which Adami was translating and arranging; consequently Puccini did not begin the composition until October 1915.

The opera was completed on 25 November 1916, the subjects of the companion-pieces being still unchosen. However, Puccini was sufficiently pleased with *Il tabarro* to consider giving it the following year in Rome as part of a double bill with *Le villi*; but the absence on military service of Titta Ruffo, his ideal Michele, caused him to abandon the idea. So *Il tabarro* waited to take its place in the *Trittico*, which had its première overseas in the composer's absence a month after the end of World War I. The first Italian production was given at the Teatro Costanzi, Rome, on 11 January 1919, under Puccini's supervision, with Maria Labia (Giorgetta), Matilde Blanco Sadun (La Frugola), Edoardo de Giovanni (Edward Johnson) (Luigi) and Carlo Galeffi (Michele); the conductor was Gino Marinuzzi and the director Tito Ricordi (son of Giulio). Late in 1921 Puccini replaced Michele's original apostrophe to the Seine ('Scorri, fiume eterno') with a brief, tauter monologue, strictly concerned with the action ('Nulla! Silenzio'), which thereafter became definitive.

*

A quay, with a barge moored alongside   Giorgetta is on deck busy with domestic chores, while her husband stands silent, gazing at the sunset. A slow, swirling theme on muted strings, touched here and there with soft woodwind notes, evokes the river Seine (it will recur constantly throughout the opera, so fixing the scene in the listener's consciousness). From time to time a ship's siren sounds. Men pass to and from the hold carrying sacks which they unload on to the quay. Below deck the strains of a shanty can be heard. Giorgetta offers a glass of wine all round; Luigi, Tinca and Talpa gladly accept.

Luigi calls to a passing organ-grinder, who obliges by striking up a waltz in discordant 7ths (reminiscent of Stravinsky's *Petrushka*). First Tinca, then Luigi dance with Giorgetta until the reappearance of Michele pulls them up short. He pays off the organ-grinder, who departs. A ballad-seller arrives on the quay and delights the strolling *midinettes* with 'The Story of Mimì' – a sad little ditty which contains a musical reference to *La bohème*. Giorgetta converses awkwardly with Michele, whose reserve she finds vaguely disquieting. La Frugola arrives in search of her husband, Talpa. She carries a sack full of odds and ends scavenged from the streets, including a titbit for her cat Caporale, the perfect companion of her solitude, and she chatters cheerfully about her activities to a modal melody accompanied by parallel common chords ('Se tu sapessi'). Talpa and the men return, having finished their work. Tinca goes off to a tavern to drown his sorrows, caused by an unfaithful wife. His mocking laughter prompts Luigi to a passionate 'declamato', a tirade against the hardships of a stevedore's life ('Hai ben ragione'). La Frugola dreams of a cottage in the country with her husband, basking in the sun and Caporale curled up at her feet ('Ho sognato una casetta'). Giorgetta longs for the happy bustle of the Parisian suburb where she was born. In her lyrical outburst ('È ben altro il mio sogno') she is joined by Luigi, who conjures up similar memories. Talpa and La Frugola retire still absorbed in their pastoral idyll, leaving Luigi and Giorgetta alone together.

At once the atmosphere becomes electric. A tense dialogue proceeds over a tremolando on the violins and a bass ostinato, broken off as Michele appears from the hold, surprised to find Luigi still there. The young man requests to be put off at Rouen, but Michele persuades him to remain aboard. No sooner has her husband gone than Giorgetta asks Luigi why he wanted to leave them. He replies that he cannot bear the thought of sharing her with someone else. They arrange a tryst for that night, the signal for which will be, as usual, a lighted match. The feeling of unbearable tension is heightened by recurrences of an upward-darting figure first heard on the horn. In a final access of passion Luigi declares that he would sooner stab her to the heart than lose her to another man. When he has gone

Giorgetta reflects miserably on the difficulty of finding true happiness. The ostinato figure dissolves into the rocking motion of the Seine theme as Michele returns, and in the course of a long *scène à deux* permeated by a new warmth, melodic and harmonic, he tries to reawaken his wife's affection for him. He recalls the child, now dead, whose cradle they used to tend, and how when the nights were cold he used to enfold them in his cloak (*tabarro*) – and here a faintly sinister motif is heard. He asks Giorgetta why she now seems never to sleep at night and she replies that the air of the cabin suffocates her; she must go on deck to breathe. For the last time Michele begs her to remain with him that night, but she evades his embrace and goes below. Michele utters one word – 'Whore!' A pair of lovers are heard singing in the distance; a bugle call from the barracks sounds the last post; then all is silence. Michele wonders who the adulterer can be. Talpa? Too old. Tinca? Always drunk. Luigi? No, he asked to leave them at Rouen. Still brooding, Michele takes out his pipe and begins to light it. Seeing the flame, which he takes to be the agreed signal, Luigi hastens aboard. To a volley of action music based on the motif first heard when the cloak is mentioned, Michele seizes him by the throat, forces him to admit that he is Giorgetta's lover, then strangles him and wraps the body in his cloak. Giorgetta returns penitent at having caused her husband pain. Timidly she begs him to take her once more within his cloak. She remembers a saying of his: 'Every one of us wears a cloak that hides sometimes a joy, sometimes a sorrow'. 'Sometimes a crime!', Michele cries, opening the garment. Giorgetta screams as Luigi's body rolls at her feet. Michele grasps her by the neck and forces her face against that of the corpse.

*

Of the three works that make up the *Trittico*, *Il tabarro* is the one most frequently performed today. Although it was composed long after the *verismo* movement of the 1890s had run its course, it approaches the canons of literary realism more closely than any of its Italian predecessors, if only by reason of its comparative restraint. The element of Grand Guignol, so blatant in Gold's play, with its double murder, is here softened. *Il tabarro* is arguably the best integrated of Puccini's scores. By far the greater part of it is cast in variants of triple or compound duple rhythm, thereby permitting the Seine theme from the beginning to surface at any point in the action without incongruity. If the lyrical moments are few, they are the more telling for their rarity.

J.B.

Suor Angelica
('Sister Angelica')

Opera in one act set to a libretto by Giovacchino Forzano; first performed in New York, at the Metropolitan Opera, on 14 December 1918 (as the second part of *Il trittico*).

At the première Geraldine Farrar was Sister Angelica, Flora Perini the Princess; the conductor was Roberto Moranzoni.

Sister Angelica	soprano
The Princess *her aunt*	contralto
The Abbess	mezzo-soprano
The Monitress	mezzo-soprano
The Mistress of the novices	mezzo-soprano
Sister Genovieffa	soprano
Sister Osmina	soprano
Sister Dolcina	soprano
The nursing sister	mezzo-soprano
The alms sisters	sopranos
The novices	sopranos
The lay sisters	soprano/mezzo-soprano

Offstage chorus of women, children and men

Setting A convent, towards the end of the 17th century

Forzano's drama about a nun who takes her own life on hearing of the death of her child had originally been planned as a spoken play. In the winter of 1916–17 he offered it to Puccini for his projected 'triptych' (*Il trittico*). The composer accepted without hesitation, despite its close resemblance to Giordano's *Mese Mariano* of 1910. Composition proceeded swiftly through the spring and summer of 1917. For local colour Puccini turned to his sister Igenia, Mother Superior at the covent at Vicepelago, and was permitted to visit her establishment and play the score to the assembled nuns, all of whom were moved to tears. Another valuable source of information was

Puccini's lifelong friend, the priest Father Pietro Panichelli, who supplied the text for what the composer flippantly referred to as the 'Marcia reale della Madonna' of the final scene.

The work was completed on 14 September 1917 and was first given along with its two companion-pieces, *Il tabarro* and *Gianni Schicchi*, the following year in America. In the meantime Puccini had extended Angelica's aria, 'Senza mamma, bimbo, tu sei morto' (Without your mother, child, you died') over a reprise of the long orchestra-based melody that heralds the arrival of the Princess's carriage; but this was not heard until the Italian premiÈre (11 January 1919), at the Teatro Costanzi, Rome under Gino Marinuzzi with Gilda dalla Rizza as Angelica and Matilde Blanco Sadun as her antagonist. In subsequent performances Gilda dalla Rizza regularly cut a short aria sung by Angelica as she gathers the flowers from which she distils the poison for her suicide, 'Amici fiori, voi mi compensate' – a remarkably modern piece with polyonal implications. Puccini eventually replaced it with a 16-bar extension of the preceding intermezzo, over which the soprano sings an altered text containing an ironical reference to the 'wasp' episode, oddly indicated in the present score as an optional cut. The aria can still be heard, though dimly, on a recording made by Lotte Lehmann in 1920. The only printed score to carry it is the first edition (1918) of the entire *Trittico*.

*

The garden of the cloister   It is a fine spring evening and the air is full of birdsong. From the chapel come the strains of an *Ave Maria*, in which Angelica's voice can be distinguished. As the nuns emerge into the garden the Monitress assigns condign punishment to two late-comers, to one Sister Lucilla for causing laughter during the service and to Sister Osmina for concealing red roses within her habit. The nuns proceed to disport themselves. Sister Genovieffa notices that the fountain is about to be turned to gold by the rays of the setting sun – a sign of divine grace, says the Monitress, that occurs only on three evenings during May. An air of melancholy descends as they remember the Sister who died a year ago. Surely, Genovieffa exclaims, her spirit would desire a libation from the gilded fountain. In a brief cantabile ('I desideri sono i fiori dei vivi') Angelica declares that desires flower only for the living; those of the dead are fulfilled before they can utter them. The Monitress maintains that to nuns all desires are forbidden; but Sister Genovieffa disagrees. Brought up as a shepherdess she yearns to fondle a pet lamb ('Soave Signor mio'). Sister Dolcina too has a wish – the sisters reply, laughing, that her wish is for some tasty morsel. And Sister Angelica? She denies wishing for anything. The sisters murmur, shocked, that that is untrue. They know that she is consumed by longing for news of the noble family that has mysteriously forced her to take the veil.

The Nursing Sister hurries in much distressed. One of the sisters has been stung by a wasp and is in agony. Angelica swiftly prepares a floral remedy and the Nursing Sister retires, praising Angelica's skill. Two Alms Sisters enter with donkey and cart and distribute provisions. The harmonic movement comes to a virtual standstill for 20 bars, until they mention having seen a magnificent coach arrive at the convent; whereupon the orchestra launches the principal melody of the opera, a long, sustained cantilena over which the voices chatter at first casually, then with growing excitement, Angelica showing particular agitation. The nuns go into the cloister as the Abbess comes to summon Angelica to meet an important visitor. The Princess enters, a formidable personage dressed in black and leaning on an ebony stick. Her frigid demeanour is conveyed in the music by a bleak unison figure that winds upward and comes to rest on an unrelated chord. She has come to ask Angelica to sign away her share of her parents' heritage to a younger sister, who is about to be married – to a man who can overlook the dishonour that Angelica has brought upon their family. Angelica protests that her aunt is inexorable. Deeply offended, the Princess tells of frequent visits to her own sister's grave, where their spirits commune ('Nel silenzio di quei raccoglimenti'). But always her thoughts return to her niece's sin and the need for its expiation.

Angelica, duly humble, insists nonetheless that she will never forget her beloved child, only to be brutally told that he has died of a fever. She collapses sobbing, but recovers sufficiently to sign the parchment and when her aunt has left pours out her grief in the aria 'Senza mamma, bimbo, tu sei morto'. Singing of divine grace ('La grazia Ë discesa dal cielo') the nuns proceed to their cells followed by Angelica, who presently reappears carrying a jar into which she pours a lethal draught distilled from flowers. Bidding the sisters a tender farewell she drinks the poison and is immediately overcome by guilt at having committed mortal sin. She prays frantically for salvation; the doors of the chapel open revealing a host of angels. In their midst is the Virgin Mary leading Angelica's child by the hand towards the dying mother, as the 'Royal March of the Madonna' swells to a climax.

*

In the dismemberment of the *Trittico* which followed the early performances, *Suor Angelica* was the first to be discarded (much to the annoyance of Puccini, who claimed it as his favourite among the three). Managements were put off by the problems of an all-female cast. Protestant audiences were alienated by the subject. Even in Italy the prevailing sweetness of the idiom held little appeal for a generation familiar with the explorations of Pizzetti and Malipiero into the austere ecclesiastical traditions of the past. Finally it may be questioned whether Puccini rose adequately to the challenge of the culminating miracle, which ideally calls for the kind of transfiguration that lay outside his range.

J.B.

Gianni Schicchi

Opera in one act set to a libretto by Giovacchino Forzano after a passage from Dante Alighieri's narrative poem *Commedia*, part 1: Inferno; first performed in New York, at the Metropolitan Opera House, on14 December 1918 (as the final part of *Il trittico*).

The cast at the première included Giuseppe De Luca Schicchi), Florence Easton (Lauretta), Giulio Crimi (Rinuccio), Kathleen Howard (Zita) and Adam Didur (Simone); the conductor was Roberto Moranzoni.

Gianni Schicchi *(aged 50)*	baritone
Lauretta *his daughter (aged 21)*	soprano
Zita *cousin of Buoso Donati (aged 60)*	contralto
Rinuccio *Zita's nephew (aged 24)*	tenor
Gherardo *Buoso's nephew (aged 40)*	tenor
Nella *Gherardo's wife (aged 34)*	soprano
Gherardino *their son (aged 7)*	contralto
Betto di Signa *Buoso's brother-in-law (of uncertain age)*	bass
Simone *cousin of Buoso (aged 70)*	bass
Marco *Simone's son*	baritone
La Ciesca *Marco's wife (aged 38)*	mezzo-soprano
Maestro Spinelloccio *a doctor*	bass
Ser Amantio di Niolao *a notary*	baritone
Pinellino *a cobbler*	bass
Guccio *a dyer*	bass

Setting Florence, 1299

Authorities disagree as to whether Puccini or Forzano first had the idea of basing a comedy on a brief passage in Canto 30 of Dante's *Inferno* concerning a sly rogue who cheated the poet's own relatives by marriage out of a substantial inheritance. Forzano submitted his scheme in March 1917 and completed the libretto in June. Puccini began work on it immediately, before laying it aside to finish the second part of *Il trittico, Suor Angelica*. The autograph is dated 3 February 1918. The Italian première took place on 11 January 1919 (Rome, Teatro Costanzi), conducted by Gino Marinuzzi, Carlo Galeffi took the title role with Edoardo Di Giovanni (Edward Johnson) as Rinuccio and Gilda dalla Rizza as Lauretta. Of the three operas that make up *Il trittico, Gianni Schicchi* won the readiest acceptance both at home and abroad though it was later to be rivalled by *Il tabarro*. It remains nonetheless among the acknowledged masterpieces of Italian comedy.

*

A bedroom in the house of Buoso Donati   Before a large four-poster bed, whose curtains conceal the body of Buoso Donati, recently defunct, Donati's relatives are kneeling in a state of well-simulated grief. The air is filled with their sobs and groans, which give way to anxious whisperings when Betto mentions a rumour that the deceased has left all his property to the Monastery of San Reparata. They turn for guidance to Simone, as he is the oldest member present and a former mayor of Fucecchio. He suggests that they search for the will immediately. All begin frantically emptying drawers and cabinets. The parchment is found by Rinuccio, but before handing it over to his aunt Zita as head of the family he makes her promise, should the terms prove satisfactory, to allow his marriage with Lauretta, daughter of Gianni Schicchi. A broad theme, evolving in lyrical sequences, indicates the warmth of Rinuccio's feelings (ex.1). Rinuccio bribes Gherardino to fetch Schicchi and the girl. Meanwhile, as the relatives gather round Zita to read the will, their expressions slowly change from eager anticipation to dismay and finally to fury, as they discover that the rumour was all too well founded. They launch into a tirade against the monks, picturing them pointing the

Ex.1 Allegro

finger of scorn at the impoverished Donati family. If only the will could be changed! But this time Simone cannot help.

Rinuccio suggests that they seek advice from Gianni Schicchi, but by now Zita will not even hear his name mentioned. Gherardino returns to tell them that Schicchi is on his way. Annoyance all round: the man is a mere parvenu, a peasant from the backwoods. Rinuccio springs to his defence in an aria ('Avete torto') which introduces a motif to be associated with Schicchi's cunning, and whose concluding section ('Firenze è come un albero fiorito'), marked 'to be sung in the manner of a Tuscan *stornello* [folksong]', compares Florence to a tree that draws its sustenance from the surrounding countryside. Schicchi arrives with his daughter, astonished to find the family plunged in genuine grief, until he learns that they have been disinherited. A quarrel breaks out between him and Zita, to the chagrin of Lauretta and Rinuccio, who see their hopes of marriage fading (the theme of ex.1 recurs in elegiac vein). Rinuccio begs Schicchi to help them, but in vain, and it is Lauretta who carries the day with her desperate plea, 'O mio babbino caro' ('Oh my beloved daddy') – the score's one detachable number, whose opening theme has been anticipated by the orchestra during Rinuccio's *stornello* as symbolizing the glories of Florence.

After sending his daughter out to the terrace Schicchi proceeds to give his instructions. Buoso's body must be removed and the bed remade. There is a knock at the door and Schicchi slips behind the curtains as Spinelloccio, the doctor, enters and asks after his patient. Imitating Buoso's voice Schicchi declares that he is much recovered and asks him to call again that evening. The doctor leaves, well pleased with the effect of his past ministrations. After a crow of triumph Schicchi unfolds his plan in an aria ('Si corre dal notaio'). Rinuccio must summon a lawyer and two witnesses; he himself will dress up in Buoso's nightgown and bonnet and dictate a new will leaving everything to the family. Delighted, they discuss the division of the property. There is perfect agreement until they reach the most valuable part of the legacy: the villa, the mule and the mills at Signa. Before the issue can be settled there is a brief alarm as a funeral bell tolls from nearby. They wonder whether news of Buoso's death can have broken, but the tolling turns out to have been for the butler of a wealthy neighbour. Amid general relief they decide to leave the allocation of the coveted items to Schicchi himself, but as they file past him, each handing him an article of clothing, they offer him bribes, all of which he pretends to accept. In a lyrical trio ('Spogliati, bambolino') Zita, Nella and La Ciesca assist him to change clothes. Before retiring behind the curtains he makes them repeat after him the penalty meted out to all who are party to the falsification of a will: namely to have their hands cut off and to be banished from the city. Obediently they chant a mock lament ('Addio Firenze, addio, cielo divino').

Rinuccio arrives with the lawyer, Ser Amantio, and two witnesses, Guccio and Pinellino. The formalities are gone through, amid universal praise for 'Buoso's' generosity. All hold their breath as he reaches the villa, the mule and the mills. These, in succession, are left to 'my dear, devoted and much loved friend, Gianni Schicchi'. The family react with smouldering rage, but, as Schicchi's intermittent chanting of 'Addio, Firenze' reminds them, they are hardly in a position to protest. Only when the lawyer and witnesses have departed do they burst out, rampaging through the house and seizing everything they can lay their hands on, until Schicchi drives them away. The lovers, on the other hand, are perfectly happy, for now that Lauretta is assured of a dowry there can be no obstacle to their marriage – the theme of ex.1 is heard in radiant mood. And Gianni Schicchi feels justified in asking the audience's indulgence, to a recurrence of the motif associated with his cunning.

*

As early as *La bohème* (1896) Puccini had shown a gift for robust comedy, with which he never failed to leaven his most pathetic plots. In *Gianni Schicchi* this style appears refined and concentrated. Verbal inflection here is as pointed as in Verdi's *Falstaff*; but the organization remains based on recurrent orchestral motifs, mostly sharp and piquant, often lacking precise associations but always sure in their theatrical effect. The harmonic idiom comprises rows of parallel dissonances, as in the scene with Spinelloccio, together with passages of bland, schoolroom diatonicism, as in the reading of the will as well as chattering reminiscences of *opera buffa*. Lauretta's aria, by far the best known in the entire *Trittico* is sometimes condemned as a concession to popular taste, but its position at the turning point of the action is precisely calculated so as to provide a welcome moment of lyrical repose.

J.B.

Turandot

Dramma lirico in three acts set to a libretto by Giuseppe Adami and Renato Simoni after Carlo Gozzi's dramatic fairy-tale; first performed in Milan, at the Teatro alla Scala, on 25 April 1926.

The outstanding first cast included Miguel Fleta (Calaf), Rosa Raisa (Turandot), Maria Zamboni (Liù), Carlo Walter (Timur) and Giacomo Rimini (Ping).

Princess Turandot	soprano
The Emperor Altoum *her father*	tenor
Timur *the dispossessed King of Tartary*	bass
Calaf *his son*	tenor
Liù *a young slave-girl*	soprano
Ping *Grand Chancellor*	baritone
Pang *General Purveyor* *(Masks)*	tenor
Pong *Chief Cook*	tenor
A Mandarin	baritone
The Prince of Persia	silent role
The Executioner (Pu-Tin-Pao)	silent role

Imperial guards, the executioner's men, boys, priests, mandarins, dignitaries, eight wise men, Turandot's handmaids, soldiers, standard-bearers, musicians, ghosts of suitors and a crowd

Setting Peking, in legendary times

The notion of basing an opera on Gozzi's most celebrated *fiaba* (fairy-tale) – one that should 'modernize and bring human warmth to the old cardboard figures' – arose during a meeting in Milan between Puccini, Adami and Simoni in winter 1919–20. Adami supplied the composer with a copy of Schiller's adaptation of the play in the Italian translation of Andrea Maffei. Puccini returned it to him with the instruction to make it the basis of the libretto, adding 'but on it you must rear another figure; I mean – I can't explain!' (clearly he was groping his way towards the conception of the slave-girl Liù). His first instinct was to exclude Gozzi's 'masks' but almost immediately afterwards he wrote: 'It is just possible that by retaining them *with discretion* we should have an Italian element which, in the midst of so much Chinese mannerism . . . would introduce a touch of our life and, above all, of sincerity'. By August 1920 the poets' original scheme had been reworked to Puccini's temporary satisfaction. Of the three acts, the first was to end with Calaf's solving of the riddles and his offer to release Turandot from her obligation provided she could find out who he is. The second would begin with her attempts to do so, including the interrogation and torture of Liù, and end with a long duet, at the climax of which Calaf would reveal his name and thus apparently seal his own fate. Act 3 would open with the preparations for Calaf's execution. At the last moment Turandot would deny all knowledge of his identity and proclaim her love for him. By the beginning of 1921 Puccini had already begun sketching the music with the help of a Chinese musical box belonging to his friend Baron Fassani and some folk music supplied by the firm of Ricordi.

Meanwhile, of the two librettists Adami seems to have assumed the usual role of Luigi Illica, working out the dialogue, and Simoni that of Giacosa, versifying the result. By September Puccini was convinced that the last two acts should be run together, so as to avoid a slackening of interest after the riddle scene. The librettists, however, were against a two-act format; and in December it was decided to bring down the curtain on Act 1 at the point where Calaf, not dissuaded by Timur, Liù and the masks, strikes the gong that announces his challenge. During the early months of 1922 Puccini worked on a new scene for the masks which would open the second act. In October he was engaged with Turandot's aria, 'In questa reggia', which follows. In November, after briefly reverting to the idea of an opera in two acts, Puccini took the unfortunate decision to have Liù die under torture. For the next two years the final duet between Calaf and Turandot proved the great obstacle. None of the versions supplied by Simoni satisfied him. By the time of his death on 29 November 1924 only a few scarcely legible sketches for it existed. At Toscanini's suggestion these were handed over to Franco

Alfano for completion. But at the première 17 months later, Toscanini laid down his baton after the death of Liù, the last music composed by Puccini. The score was published with Alfano's ending, shortened in a second edition (the one in regular use). Alfano's conclusion (which has since been given in full in concert performance) fails to redeem the inevitable anticlimax. Clearly the man who can persist in his wooing of a woman of whom he knows nothing, and whom he has every reason to dislike, immediately after a slave-girl has killed herself for his sake, is bound to forfeit our sympathy. Puccini hoped that the librettists would be able to solve the problem for him; but even if they had succeeded it is likely that, as in *Suor Angelica*, he would not have found the appropriate note of transfiguration on which to end.

The title role is one of the supreme challenges for a dramatic soprano. Outstanding exponents have included Claudia Muzio, Lotte Lehmann, Maria Jeritza, Maria Németh, Eva Turner and, later, Maria Callas, Birgit Nilsson and Gwyneth Jones.

*

ACT 1 *A public square in Peking beneath the city ramparts, with the imperial palace to one side* From a bastion a Mandarin proclaims the Emperor's decree: the Princess Turandot shall wed the first suitor of royal lineage who succeeds in solving her three riddles; all who fail will be executed. The Prince of Persia 'whom fortune has not favoured' is due to be beheaded when the moon rises. The crowd surges forward in eager anticipation, only to be brutally repulsed by the imperial guards. As their shouts turn to groans and lamentations, the stark, bitonal flourishes of the orchestra give way to a broad, characteristically Puccinian, drooping melody. In the scrimmage an old blind man is knocked to the ground. The girl accompanying him calls for help. Their rescuer is the disguised Prince Calaf, who recognizes the old man as his father, Timur, exiled King of Tartary. Both are in flight from their country's enemies. Timur's companion is the slave-girl Liù, who decided to share the family's sufferings when Calaf bestowed a smile on her long ago. The hectic motion is resumed as the Executioner's men arrive and begin sharpening the axe. The general blood-lust is conveyed in a fierce ostinato of varied phrase-lengths, yielding to a mood of rapt reverie as all pray for the moon to appear. Slowly the scene fills with a silvery light, reflected in a diaphanous tissue of harmony and scoring. As the culminating cry of 'Pu-Tin-Pao' (the Executioner) subsides, a chorus of boys is heard approaching. Their chant ('Là, sui monti dell'est') is a version of the Chinese folksong 'Moo-Lee-Vha' and will stand for Turandot in her official capacity. Next comes the procession that escorts the Prince of Persia to the scaffold (here Puccini uses a modal idiom with sharpened 4th). The young man's looks and dignified bearing move the crowd to pity and they call on the Princess to spare his life, but she confirms his sentence with a silent gesture and the procession moves on.

Timur, Calaf and Liù are left alone in the square. From far off the Prince of Persia invokes the name of Turandot as the axe falls. But Calaf has been so overwhelmed by the Princess's beauty that he is determined to try his fortune with her, despite his father's remonstrances. He is about to strike the gong and issue his challenge when the masks, Ping, Pang and Pong, rush in and restrain him. To fragments of the Chinese national hymn set out in alternations of duple and triple time, they try to deflect Calaf from his purpose. From the balcony the Princess's handmaidens call for silence – their mistress is sleeping. The masks pay no heed and continue their persuasions. The ghosts of former suitors materialize on the battlements, each bewailing his unrequited love. The masks point to where the Executioner appears bearing the Prince of Persia's severed head. Timur joins his plea to theirs. In her pentatonic arietta ('Signore, ascolta') Liù makes a last appeal, to which Calaf, deeply moved, replies ('Non piangere, Liù'), recommending Timur to her care should he himself fail the test. As he continues to hold out, the music develops into a broadly swaying tug-of-war based on alternating chords and reinforced by the full chorus singing offstage. At the climax Calaf strikes the gong three times. Liù and Timur are in despair.

ACT 2 scene i *A pavilion* Ping, Pang and Pong are preparing for either eventuality – a wedding or a funeral. They reflect on China's misery ever since Turandot came to power. From ministers of state they have become servants of the Executioner. In an andantino of nostalgia ('Ho una casa nell'Honan') each recalls his home in the peace of the countryside. Memories of Turandot's past victims, evoked by an unseen chorus, give way to hopes that the man has been found who can tame her and restore tranquillity to the land. To the sound of trumpets the palace wakes to life, and the music continues without a break into scene ii.

ACT 2 scene ii   *The palace courtyard*   Gradually a crowd assembles. The various dignitaries take their places, among them the eight wise men, each bearing three scrolls. High up on an ivory throne sits the Emperor Altoum. In an old man's quavering voice he tries in vain to dissuade Calaf from his enterprise. A solemn choral hymn wishes him 10,000 years of life. Once again the Mandarin reads aloud the imperial decree regarding the Princess; and again the unseen boys' chorus is heard, a prelude to the appearance of Turandot herself. Her show-stopping aria 'In questa reggia' tells the story of her ancestress Lo-u Ling, who was ravished and murdered by a foreign army, and whose memory she has sworn to avenge on any man foolhardy enough to woo her. A pattern of three chords introduces each of her riddles, to which Calaf gives the correct answers ('Hope', 'Blood' and 'Turandot'). The music of the boys' chorus, entrusted to full chorus and orchestra, now celebrates Calaf's victory. Turandot, in great distress, begs Altoum to release her from her vow, but he refuses. It is Calaf who offers her a way of escape. If by the following dawn she can discover his name, he will consent to be beheaded. Everyone hails Altoum, who hopes to be able to welcome Calaf as his son-in-law.

ACT 3 scene i   *The palace gardens, at night*   Distant heralds repeat the Princess's command that none shall sleep on pain of death until the Prince's name be revealed. In his celebrated *romanza* 'Nessun dorma', whose principal strain testifies to Puccini's undiminished lyrical gifts, Calaf echoes their words, resolving that his secret shall never be disclosed. The three masks emerge from the shrubbery and offer Calaf various bribes – young half-naked girls, jewels, promises of renown – but he rejects them all. The crowd that has meantime gathered menace him with their daggers, when suddenly the imperial guards appear dragging in Timur and Liù, who were spotted with Calaf. The Princess is summoned. She orders the interrogation of Timur, but it is Liù who steps forward, claiming that she alone knows the Prince's name. Turandot has her bound and Ping tries to make her talk. In words of Puccini's own devising Liù tells the mystified Princess that love has given her the power to resist ('Tu che di gel sei cinta'). Her mournful melody continues throughout the painful scene that follows with an insistence that recalls the roll-call of the prostitutes in *Manon Lescaut*. The Executioner arrives; he and his men torture Liù. At the end of her strength she snatches a dagger from one of the guards and stabs herself. Timur, being blind, has to be told of her death; he joins the lugubrious procession that bears her body away. At this point Alfano's reconstruction takes over, beginning with a duet ('Principessa di morte') between Calaf and Turandot, in which the Princess, at first haughty and unyielding, succumbs when Calaf embraces her. Humiliated, she begs him to leave, taking his secret with him. But he now feels sufficiently confident to tell her that he is Calaf, son of Timur. At once she recovers her pride, realizing that she still holds his life in her hands. A female chorus punctuated by brass flourishes leads into the final scene.

ACT 3 scene ii   *The palace courtyard*   Once again the Emperor, his courtiers and the people have assembled. Advancing with Calaf, Turandot declares that at last she knows his name – it is 'Love'. Chorus and orchestra unite in a triumphant reprise of the Nessun dorma' motif.

*

Despite its unfinished state *Turandot* is rightly regarded as the summit of Puccini's achievement, bearing witness to a capacity for self-renewal unsurpassed by that of still greater composers. The style remains true to the composer's 19th-century roots, but it is toughened and amplified by the assimilation of uncompromisingly modern elements, including bitonality and an adventurous use of whole-tone, pentatonic and modal harmony. The resulting synthesis commands a new range of expression (the pentatonic scale, no longer a mere orientalism as in *Madama Butterfly*, conveys the full depth of Liù's pathos in 'Signore, ascolta'). The music is organized in massive blocks, each motivically based – a system which shows to particular advantage in Act 1, arguably the most perfectly constructed act in Puccini's output; while the scoring shows a rare imagination in the handling of large forces (the writing for xylophone alone immediately attracts the attention). These attributes, combined with Puccini's unfailing ability to communicate directly with an audience, have established *Turandot* as a classic of 20th-century opera.

J.B.

Italian Contemporaries and their Operas

Alfredo Catalani

Alfredo Catalani was born in Lucca on 19 June 1854; he died in Milan, on 7 August 1893. His operas were among the most important of those in the period immediately preceding the rise of the *verismo* school.

The musical families of Lucca include the Catalani as well as the Boccherini and the Puccini. Alfredo was introduced to music by his father, and after achieving the necessary scholastic qualifications studied composition at the Istituto Pacini in Lucca under Fortunato Magi, the uncle and first teacher of Giacomo Puccini, graduating in 1872 with a prize for composition. He proceeded to the Paris Conservatoire, where he attended classes by Marmontel (piano) and Bazin (composition) and also suffered the first attacks of haemoptysis, a condition that was to overshadow his future career. At the end of 1873 he went to the Milan Conservatory to study with Bazzini. His diploma piece and first contribution to stage music was the one-act *La falce* (1875) to a libretto by Arrigo Boito, whom Catalani had met in Milan, together with Franco Faccio and Marco Praga, at the salon of Clarina Maffei. He strengthened his ties with the Milanese followers of the Scapigliatura movement, taking part in discussions of contemporary topics and sharing their interest in innovations in drama and opera, above all the aesthetics of Wagner, whose works were then frequently performed in some Italian opera houses.

Giovannina Lucca, the publisher involved at first hand in the publication of Wagner's music, commissioned from Catalani a new large-scale dramatic work, *Elda*. The libretto, by the translator Carlo d'Ormeville, was based on the legend of the Lorelei as narrated by Heine and others. The score was completed in 1876 and revised in 1877, but the work was staged at the Teatro Regio, Turin, only in 1880, through the efforts of the conductor Carlo Pedrotti and the music critic Giuseppe Depanis, who became a devoted friend.

The libretto for Catalani's next opera, *Dejanice*, was provided by another translator, Angelo Zanardini, but it was a weak neo-classical drama, coldly received at La Scala in 1883. Boito inspired the programme of Catalani's most important orchestral composition, the symphonic poem *Ero e Leandro*; it was conducted in 1885 by Faccio, who in the following February also conducted *Edmea* at La Scala. This, Catalani's fourth opera, a collaboration with Ghislanzoni, had a moderate success, repeated at the Carignano in Turin later in the same year; the conductor was Arturo Toscanini, then under 20, who was later to make Catalani's work widely known.

With only small earnings from theatrical work, Catalani applied for the post of composition professor at the Milan Conservatory left vacant by the death of Ponchielli in 1886. Although he was the outstanding candidate, his appointment was not made official until April 1888 because of doubts about his health. In the same year he lost the support of Lucca, whose firm was taken over by Ricordi. Depanis secured a successful production of the revised *Elda*, now called *Loreley*, at Turin in 1890, after a reworking of the libretto by Zanardini with help from Giuseppe Giacosa and Luigi Illica. Catalani then asked Illica to produce a libretto for *La Wally*, and when the new opera was completed he offered it to Ricordi. The publisher appreciated its qualities but stipulated a contract in which payment was to be made in three instalments, the last to be due on the 60th performance.

In spite of the successful first performance at La Scala in 1892, the opera was not often staged, while the slow but progressive worsening of Catalani's illness had intensified the persecution complex from which he suffered: he interpreted the success of other composers, more favoured by Ricordi, as a threat to his own work. He was wounded by Verdi's recommendation of Franchetti to the Genoese authorities to compose *Cristoforo Colombo*, and by the triumph of *Manon Lescaut* that marked Puccini as the legitimate successor to Verdi. His complaints at Ricordi's high-handed treatment of *La Wally* were not without justification, although criticisms he made of Puccini's music in letters were perhaps understandably unfavourable. Catalani never received the third and final instalment guaranteed by his publisher; he died on 7 August 1893 after a series of attacks of haemoptysis.

Almost all Catalani's work reflects his preference for the sort of theme favoured by the Scapigliatura, characterized by a Nordic setting in which natural elements play an important part, with suggestions of the supernatural and echoes of legend, and love romantically linked with death. *La falce*, his first and only collaboration with Boito (the most influential member of the group), cannot be called a success. Opening with an atmospheric symphonic prologue typical of the time (as in Boito's *Mefistofele* and the interlude in Puccini's *Le Villi*), the opera has an oriental flavour generically akin to that of Félicien David's *Le désert*. The plot is contrived, with a heroine morbidly attracted to a reaper who is believed to be the incarnation of Death but who instead reveals himself to be a real flesh-and-blood man. The denouement results in an unintentional, somewhat grotesque trivialization of the love-death equation, and the setting and characters are not adequately realized in the music.

When Boito refused to continue to collaborate with him, Catalani formed a partnership with d'Ormeville, who condensed the best features of the Rhinegold mythology into the text of *Elda*. The failure of the production, however, meant that Catalani's originality, his avoidance of excessive realistic contrasts by immersing the action in an atmosphere of suffused timbres and original harmonic textures, was not appreciated.

His next work, *Dejanice*, a bombastic historical drama, represented a distinct setback in his career. Zanardini was predominantly a translator of grand operas and of Wagner's works. He provided the composer with verses composed lightheartedly and with dramatic situations constituting a collection of the most famous operatic commonplaces of the day, from the neo-classical setting of *Norma* to the chorus of priestesses with dances as in *Aida*; there are also echoes of *Un ballo in maschera*, *Luisa Miller* and *L'Africaine*. The dramatic situation and its final solution are those of *La Gioconda* – a conflict between a woman who is loved (Argelia/Laura), and a loving woman (Dejanira/La Gioconda) who sacrifices herself to secure the happiness of her rival and the man she loves (Admeto/Enzo). This plot, with the variation that the voluntary victim is a man (Ulmo), was used again in *Edmea*, a more interesting opera musically because Catalani had matured considerably as a composer, and more successful, though Ghislanzoni was no better a librettist. The melodic line is more original, the Bohemian setting represented with realistic vivacity and the love drama that drives the heroine to madness happily resolved in the end.

Because of its lively dramatic style, *Edmea* pleased the public more than Catalani's other operas, and this made him realize that its formula was better suited to his abilities. On the advice of Depanis, he decided to apply this further by revising *Elda*. He restored the original names and places, wrote new passages and improved the musical quality of the existing score. The plot of the new *Loreley*, sketched out by Depanis and elaborated by Zanardini and d'Ormeville (who were helped by Illica and Giacosa, later to write librettos for Puccini), gained considerably in liveliness and interest.

Loreley was a worthy forerunner to *La Wally*, indisputedly Catalani's most successful opera. His liberation from the traditional structure of self-contained numbers, largely observed in his previous works, was mainly the result of a new conception of characterization and of atmospheric orchestral writing to act as connective tissue in the drama. If many lyrical passages, vocal and orchestral, anticipate features of *verismo*, and the harmonic organization shows that he had learnt from Wagner, Catalani's real achievement in *La Wally* is the fusion of these heterogeneous factors into a unified and original whole. He was perhaps the most authoritative musical representative of the ideals of the Scapigliatura, although he inclined equally to a decadent and twilight world, providing a glimmer of refined if anaemic originality in Italian opera as it moved away from the domination of Verdi towards *verismo* conformity. Unfortunately Catalani could not aspire to the leading role in Italian and European opera assumed by Puccini, who had greater musical gifts and outstanding dramatic talent. But though on a lower level, his works are the fruit of a similar sensitivity and permeated with a similar restlessness.

M.G.

Loreley

Azione romantica in three acts set to a libretto by Angelo Zanardini and others after Carlo d'Ormeville's libretto for Catalani's *Elda* (1880, Turin); first performed in Turin's Teatro Regio, on 16 February 1890.

*

The action takes place on the shores of the Rhine in 1300. Although he is in love with the young Loreley (soprano), Walter von Oberwesel (tenor), encouraged by his friend Baron Hermann (baritone), intends to keep his promise to marry Anna von Rehberg (soprano), niece of the Margrave of Biberich (bass). Instead of seeking revenge, Loreley offers her life to Albrich, god of the Rhine, who allows her to plunge into the river and emerge more beautiful. She appears as a mirage to Walter as the wedding is about to be celebrated, and he is overwhelmed with love for her. He leaves his bride to follow Loreley and feels remorse only when he sees the funeral procession of Anna, who has died of a broken heart. For a short time Loreley abandons herself to Walter's embrace, but the spirits remind her of her pact with the god and she bids her love farewell for ever. In despair Walter throws himself into the river to follow her.

*

A reworking of the four-act *dramma fantastico Elda*, Catalani's second opera, *Loreley*, reaches greater artistic heights because of improvements in the libretto (Zanardini, Giuseppe Depanis and d'Ormeville all contributed, along with Giuseppe Giacosa and Luigi Illica) as well as in the composer's capabilities. The third act is particularly interesting, containing some of the most important descriptive writing in the stage music of the period, such as the dance of the water-spirits and the funeral march for the dead Anna.

M.G.

La Wally

Dramma musicale in four acts set to a libretto by Luigi Illica after Wilhelmine von Hillern's story *Die Geyer-Wally*; first performed in Milan, at the Teatro alla Scala, on 20 January 1892.

*

The action takes place in the Tyrol in about 1800. In the village of Hochstoff the rich landowner Stromminger (bass) taunts Haghenbach (tenor), from the rival village of Sölden, on his return from a hunting expedition. Stromminger's daughter Wally (soprano) tries to make peace between them and sends away the young huntsman, for whom she shows an obvious partiality; this in turn annoys the factor Gellner (baritone), secretly in love with her, who reveals his feelings to the still angry Stromminger. When her father insists that she must marry Gellner, Wally refuses and he banishes her. She goes off into the mountains with her friend Walter (light soprano), and a year later returns to claim the estate she has inherited from her now deceased father. She goes to Sölden for a festival and in a fit of jealousy over Haghenbach insults Afra (mezzo-soprano), a tavern owner, having been wrongly led to believe by Gellner that Afra is betrothed to the man Wally loves. To avenge the insult, Haghenbach consents to dance with Wally and gives her a kiss, swearing falsely that he loves her. The mockery of the bystanders makes Wally aware of the truth, and she promises to marry Gellner if he will kill Haghenbach. The same evening Haghenbach, who realizes that he loves Wally, goes to Hochstoff to see her but is attacked by Gellner, who hurls him into a ravine. Wally, overcome by remorse, rushes to save him and returns him to Afra, to whom she leaves all her wealth. She goes away before the young man recovers, returning to her refuge in the mountains, and is eventually joined by Haghenbach, who tells her of his love. The couple are finally reconciled, but as they seek the path back the young man is carried away by an avalanche. Calling his name in vain, Wally flings herself into the abyss.

*

In this work, recognized as his masterpiece, Catalani shows himself halfway between *verismo* opera and Puccini (who was to triumph with *Manon* the following year) and in harmony with Italian deca-dentism, in particular the poetry of Giovanni Pascoli and Guido Gozzano. From the strictly musical point of view the opera's merits lie in its good control of orchestration and expressive melodies, and at some points the musical characterization is very successful. Its weakness is a lack of dramatic interest in the plot, the development of which is too protracted and lacking in intensity. Although it has no great or unforgettable character, dramatic intuition or linguistic craftsmanship such as there is in Puccini, the small world of *La Wally* is real and finely chiselled, and this microcosm becomes a creation worthy of a place among the operas that characterize European *fin-de-siècle* music drama.

M.G.

Francesco Cilea

Francesco Cilea was born in Palmi, Reggio Calabria, on 23 July 1866; he died in Varazze, Savona, on 20 November 1950. The son of an impoverished lawyer, he was educated at a boarding school in Naples from the age of seven.

The influence of Francesco Florimo, the famous archivist and friend of Bellini, helped him to enter the Naples Conservatory in 1879, where his teachers were Paolo Serrao, Beniamino Cesi and Giuseppe Martucci and his fellow pupils included Umberto Giordano. There he made rapid progress, becoming a *maestrino* in 1885. His Suite for Orchestra (1887) was awarded a government prize, and several of his piano pieces were published by Ricordi in Italy and Bote & Bock in Germany. His opera *Gina* was performed at the Conservatory on 9 February 1889, his final year. Despite a poor libretto, the editor Sonzogno thought sufficiently well of it to commission from Cilea an opera on a fashionable low-life subject. *La Tilda* was given with moderate success at the Teatro Pagliano, Florence, on 7 April 1892 under Rodolfo Ferrari with Fanny Torresella as protagonist. Sonzogno included it in his Italian opera season mounted later that year in Vienna, where it gained the gratifying approval of the critic Eduard Hanslick. Cilea spent three years over the composition of his next opera, *L'arlesiana*, to a libretto taken from Alphonse Daudet's play for which Bizet had provided incidental music. The text of Rosa Mamai's aria ('Esser madre è un inferno') was supplied by Grazia Pierantoni, the wife of the senator in whose house Cilea was staying at the time. The opera was well received at its première at Sonzogno's Teatro Lirico, where it helped to launch the young Caruso on his international career. Not until the following year, however, did *L'arlesiana* achieve its definitive three-act form.

In 1900 Cilea began work on his most famous opera, *Adriana Lecouvreur*, whose subject appealed to him because of its 18th-century ambience and its mixture of comedy and pathos. Its première proved another triumph for Caruso as well as for the composer. At a season of Cilea's operas launched by Sonzogno at the Théâtre Sarah

Bernhardt, Paris, in 1904, Alfred Bruneau singled out *Adriana Lecouvreur* as preferable to all other works from the Italian 'giovane scuola'. A projected collaboration with Gabriele D'Annunzio on a *Francesca da Rimini* came to nothing, owing to Sonzogno's failure to meet the poet's financial demands. In his search for a subject that would offer a choral dimension Cilea turned to *Gloria*, a story of star-crossed lovers set in 14th-century Siena at the time of the siege. Despite the advocacy of Toscanini the opera failed at its première; nor did the revised version fare substantially better. Two more abortive operatic attempts were to follow, *Ritorno ad amore* and *Il matrimonio selvaggio*. By now Cilea had effectively ceased to compose, his only other work of substance being the 'poema' *Il canto della vita*, to a text by Sem Benelli, written to commemorate the Verdi centenary in 1913. The previous year Leopoldo Mugnone had conducted a revival of *L'arlesiana* in Naples, at which he had omitted Rosa Mamai's aria and her subsequent scene with *L'Innocente*. This so incensed Cilea that he withdrew the score from circulation for the next 24 years. It would not be heard again until 1936, once more at Naples, and in 1937 in Milan, for which occasion Cilea added a prelude based on themes from the opera.

Until his retirement in 1935 Cilea pursued a distinguished career in musical education. From 1890 to 1892 he taught harmony and the piano at the Naples Conservatory; from 1896 to 1904 he held the chair of harmony and composition at the Istituto Reale (later Conservatorio) of Florence. In 1913 he assumed the directorship of the Palermo Conservatory, passing to that of the Naples Conservatory in 1916, a post which he held for nearly 20 years. He was elected to the Academy in 1938.

Of the composers of the 'giovane scuola' Cilea had a lighter, more delicate touch than most. His operas, while allowing room for the detachable number, are motivically organized, even if the motifs themselves are rarely very theatrical (the 'poison' theme in *Adriana Lecouvreur* usually passes unnoticed as such). A competent pianist, his orchestral writing frequently shows traces of piano figuration; indeed, *Adriana Lecouvreur* has been described as the best orches-tral score ever written for piano. Cilea was undoubtedly more of an

95

all-round musician than most of his contemporaries, whose interests were principally operatic. Among his gods were Paisiello and Bellini, and although his melodic style mostly conforms to the slow swirl of Mascagni and his school, it never descends to brutal excess. If *Adriana Lecouvreur* remains his most popular opera, largely through its perennial appeal to the prima donna, his best-loved single aria is 'È la solita storia del pastore' from *L'arlesiana*, which remains one of the gems of the tenor repertory.

J.B.

Adriana Lecouvreur

Francesco Cilea's opera *Adriana Lecouvreur* is set in four acts to a libretto by Arturo Colautti after Eugène Scribe and Ernest Legouvé's play *Adrienne Lecouvreur*. It was first performed in Milan, at the Teatro Lirico, on 6 November 1902.

The first cast included Enrico Caruso (Maurizio), Angelica Pandolfini (Adriana) and Giuseppe De Luca (Michonnet). The conductor was Cleofonte Campanini.

Adriana Lecouvreur of the Comédie Française	soprano
Maurizio *Count of Saxon*	tenor
Prince of Bouillon	bass
Princess of Bouillon	mezzo-soprano
Michonnet *stage director of the Comédie Française*	baritone
Quinault	bass
Poisson	tenor
Mlle Jouvenot	soprano
Mlle Dangeville	mezzo-soprano
Abbé of Chazeuil	tenor

Quinault, Poisson, Mlle Jouvenot, Mlle Dangeville } *members of the Comédie*

Ladies, gentlemen, mute extras, stage hands, valets and dancers

Setting Paris, March 1730

Adriana Lecouvreur was commissioned by the publisher Edoardo Sonzogno following the success of Cilea's *L'arlesiana*. Cilea chose the subject for its mixture of comedy and tragedy, its 18th-century ambience, the loving intensity of its protagonist and the moving final act; three other operas use the story of Adrienne Lecouvreur (by Edoardo Vera, Tommaso Benvenuti and Ettore Perosio). Colautti reduced the intricate mechanism of Scribe's plot to a serviceable operatic framework, occasionally at the expense of clarity. The première, however, was outstandingly successful.

The first London performance took place at Covent Garden in 1904 in the presence of the composer with Rina Giachetti (Adriana),

Giuseppe Anselmi (Maurizio) and Mario Sammarco (Michonnet), again under Campanini. Three years later the opera arrived at the Metropolitan Opera, New York, with Caruso (Maurizio), Lina Cavalieri (Adriana) and Antonio Scotti (Michonnet). Since then *Adriana Lecouvreur* has proved the only one of Cilea's three surviving operas to stay in the international repertory, mainly due to the opportunities it affords to an experienced prima donna who has already passed her prime. Famous among postwar exponents of the title role are Maria Caniglia, Renata Tebaldi, Magda Olivero, Renata Scotto and Joan Sutherland.

*

ACT 1   *The foyer of the Comédie Française*   The curtain is about to rise. Actors and actresses are snapping at one another and at Michonnet, who protests that he has only one pair of hands. The evening's tragedy is Corneille's *Bajazet*, featuring both Adriana and her rival Mlle Duclos. The Prince of Bouillon, La Duclos' lover, arrives with the Abbé of Chazeuil and pays affected compliments to the players. Adriana enters reading her lines; she tells her admiring hearers that she is merely the poet's handmaid ('Io son l'umile ancella'), to a melody which will serve as her theme throughout the opera. Alone with Adriana, Michonnet, who has recently come into an inheritance, is about to propose marriage to the actress, with whom he has been in love for years, when she gives him to understand that she herself loves an officer in the service of the Count of Saxony who will be in the theatre that night. But the man who now enters is Maurizio, the Count himself, who is wooing Adriana under a false identity. In a brief solo, 'La dolcissima effigie sorridente', he pours out his feelings for her. A love duet develops, after which Adriana leaves to go on stage, having given Maurizio a nosegay of violets and agreed to meet him after the performance. Meanwhile the Abbé has managed to intercept a letter addressed to Maurizio from, as he thinks, La Duclos arranging a tryst for that evening at the love-nest by the Seine in which the Prince has installed her. The Prince decides to surprise the guilty pair by organizing a party in the same house at the appointed hour. Receiving the letter, Maurizio is well aware that the writer is not La Duclos but the Princess of Bouillon, whose lover he has been in the past, and he decides for political reasons to keep the assignation. He therefore has a note conveyed to Adriana breaking their appointment. Adriana is duly upset; but on being invited to join the Prince's party, at which, she is told, the Count of Saxony himself will be one of the guests, she consents to come in order to have the opportunity of furthering her lover's career.

ACT 2 *Mlle Duclos' villa by the Seine* The Princess is waiting anxiously for Maurizio ('Acerba voluttà, dolce tortura'). When he arrives she notices the nosegay and at once suspects another woman. With great presence of mind he offers it to her. She tells him that she has spoken on his behalf to the Queen of France, but finds his gratitude inadequate. Reluctantly he admits to another liaison. At the sound of a second carriage arriving she darts into the adjoining room. The Prince and the Abbé enter laughing and congratulate Maurizio on his latest conquest, whom they take to be La Duclos. Maurizio, grasping the situation, decides to keep up the deception. Adriana arrives, to be made aware for the first time of her lover's true identity. Their duet of happiness is interrupted by Michonnet, who has come with a message for La Duclos. He is told by the Abbé that she is somewhere in the villa, whereupon Adriana assumes that Maurizio has come for a secret rendezvous with her; but this he solemnly denies. There is indeed a woman in the next room, he says, with whom his relations are purely political. Adriana must see to it that no one enters that room and, once the guests have gone in to supper, must extinguish the lights and help the unknown visitor to escape in the dark. Adriana follows his instructions. However, the few words exchanged between the women in darkness make it apparent that both are in love with Maurizio. As lights are seen approaching Adriana determines to expose her rival. But the Princess has escaped, dropping a bracelet, which Michonnet picks up and hands to Adriana.

ACT 3 *The Palais Bouillon* Preparations for a party are in train, under the supervision of the Abbé, who flirts discreetly with the Princess until her husband joins them. An amateur chemist, he has discovered a poisonous powder which, when inhaled, will induce delirium followed by death. (All this he describes to the Abbé and the Princess in a passage cut from certain editions of the opera.) Adriana arrives without her jewellery, which she has pawned in order to effect the release of Maurizio, imprisoned by order of the jealous Princess. Seeming to recognize her voice as that of her rival, the Princess lays a trap for Adriana. She tells her that Maurizio has been fatally wounded in a duel. The actress duly comes over faint; but she revives spectacularly when Maurizio himself enters and entertains the guests with tales of his military exploits ('Il russo Mencikoff'). A company of dancers perform *The Judgment of Paris*. In the general conversation that follows the Princess and Adriana fence with each other verbally. The Princess mentions a nosegay of violets. Adriana produces the compromising bracelet which the Prince identifies as his wife's. To distract attention the Princess proposes that the great actress should recite from one of her famous roles. At the Prince's suggestion she chooses a passage from Racine's *Phèdre*, where the heroine denounces lustful women; and as she declaims the lines she looks straight at her rival. All applaud her performance except the Princess who, white with fury, determines on revenge.

ACT 4 *Adriana's house* It is her birthday, but convinced that Maurizio no longer loves her Adriana has retired into solitude. Michonnet visits her in a vain attempt to bring her comfort. They are joined by four of her fellow artists, each with a present for her. Michonnet too offers a gift – Adriana's jewellery which he has redeemed with the inheritance from his uncle. Deeply touched, Adriana declares that she will return to the stage. Her colleagues entertain her with a gossipy madrigal. The maid comes in with a package labelled 'from Maurizio'. While the actors retire Adriana opens it and finds inside the nosegay of violets she had given him, now withered – a sign, she thinks, that their love is at an end. She pours out her grief in the aria 'Poveri fiori'; then she presses the flowers to her lips and throws them into the fire. But Michonnet has already summoned Maurizio, who now arrives, protests his undying devotion and offers her his hand in marriage. Adriana joyfully accepts, then suddenly turns pale. Her mind starts to wander. Clearly the nosegay was sprinkled with the poisonous powder, sent not by Maurizio but by the Princess. Adriana tries desperately to cling to life, but she is beyond help and dies in Maurizio's arms.

*

The texture of *Adriana Lecouvreur* is more richly woven and the style somewhat less emphatic than in most *verismo* operas of the time. The ensemble scenes, especially in Act 1, owe something to Verdi's *Falstaff*, though the orchestral figuration is often curiously pianistic. Use is made of recurring motifs, several of which anticipate the solos from which they derive. Some (e.g. that of the violets) are insufficiently theatrical for their associations to register. There are touches of period stylization in the dances of Act 3, but in the main Cilea is content to evoke a generalized elegance, varied by characteristic moments of lyrical effusion. Particularly effective is his recourse to unsung speech to point up Adriana's recitation at the end of the third act.

J.B.

Umberto Giordano

Umberto Menotti Maria Giordano was born in Foggia on 28 August 1867; he died in Milan on 12 November 1948. The son of a chemist who intended him for the career of a fencing master, he devoted himself to music against his parents' will. In 1882 he was admitted to the Naples Conservatory, where his teachers included Paolo Serrao and Giuseppe Martucci.

While still a student he entered a one-act opera, *Marina*, for the Sonzogno competition of 1889. Although short-listed among the 73 submissions it was awarded only sixth place (the winner being Mascagni with *Cavalleria rusticana*). Nonetheless Sonzogno thought sufficiently well of it to commission from Giordano a full-length opera, *Mala vita* (1892, Rome), based on a novella of low-life in Naples by Salvatore Di Giacomo. With its wealth of local colour and strong story line it proved highly successful in Austria and Germany, where it began a temporary vogue for operas in a Neapolitan setting. In Italy it was found too shocking, and five years later Giordano revised it as *Il voto*, without beneficial results. However, following Ricordi's example with Puccini, Sonzogno provided Giordano with a monthly stipend against the composition of his next opera. This was *Regina Diaz* (1894, Naples), intended for the celebrations of Mercadante's centenary. The subject (essentially that of Donizetti's *Maria di Rohan*) failed to inspire the composer; and the opera was withdrawn after the second performance. As a result, Edoardo Sonzogno decided to withhold Giordano's retainer, but he was persuaded otherwise by Alberto Franchetti, who ceded the libretto of *Andrea Chénier* to his younger colleague.

That same year Giordano settled in Milan, where he married Olga Spatz-Wurms, whose family owned the hotel in which Verdi regularly stayed during his last years – a circumstance which enabled the younger composer to make his acquaintance and receive from him valuable advice. The success of *Andrea Chénier* (1896, Milan) established Giordano in the front rank of the 'giovane scuola'. He then returned to a long-cherished project of an opera based on Sardou's

Fedora, which was launched at Sonzogno's Teatro Lirico in 1898. This too was destined to remain in the repertory. A third triumph, though more temporary, followed with *Siberia* (1903, Milan), after which Giordano's fortunes declined. *Marcella* (1907, Milan), a story of love and renunciation across the class barrier, failed, as did *Mese Mariano* (1910, Palermo), in which Giordano returned to Di Giacomo; the plot of *Mese Mariano* anticipates to a surprising extent that of Puccini's *Suor Angelica*. Following an old suggestion of Verdi that he write an opera showing Napoleon *en pantoufles* he turned to Sardou's comedy *Madame Sans-Gêne* (1915, New York). Owing to the outbreak of war the première was given in his absence with a cast that included Geraldine Farrar, Giovanni Zenatello and Pasquale Amato; the conductor was Toscanini. But this too made little impression. Together with Franchetti he wrote an operetta, *Giove a Pompei* (1921, Rome), his own contribution having been mostly composed 20 years earlier.

Then came an unexpected success, *La cena delle beffe* (1924, Milan), written to a libretto by Sem Benelli, adapted (with the help of Giovacchino Forzano) from his own gruesome play set in Florence during the reign of Lorenzo the Magnificent. Held by some to be Giordano's dramatic masterpiece, the opera is still occasionally revived. His last work for the stage was the one-act *Il re* (1929, Milan), a lighthearted moralistic fantasy by Forzano composed as a vehicle for the coloratura soprano, Toti Dal Monte. Under Toscanini it enjoyed a certain vogue during the 1930s with Maria Caniglia and Lina Pagliughi as well as Dal Monte. A ballet, *L'astro magico*, remained unperformed, while an opera to a libretto by Forzano on the subject of Rasputin never materialized.

Although he showed no great individuality as a melodist, Giordano handled the late Romantic, emotionally vehement idiom of the 'giovane scuola' with ease and fluency, being particularly skilful in weaving into his textures elements of local and historical colour – Neapolitan dance rhythms (*Mala vita*), French Revolutionary songs (*Andrea Chénier* and *Madame Sans-Gêne*), Russian folk music (*Siberia*), 18th-century pastiche (*Chénier*), pseudo-Chopin piano music and Swiss *ranz des vaches* (*Fedora*). Musically his operas are

103

more loosely organized than those of his Italian contemporaries, with sparing use of recurring themes. His largest-scale work is *Siberia*. In his later operas the somewhat crude scoring gives way to a more refined technique, which yields telling results in *La cena delle beffe*, even if the subject could be thought to require a more astringent musical vocabulary. His stage sense is always sure, and his vocal writing unfailingly effective. *Andrea Chénier* owes its place in the repertory to the unusual opportunities it offers to a star tenor.

J.B.

Andrea Chénier

Dramma istorico in four acts ('tableaux') set to a libretto by Luigi Illica; first performed in Milan, at the Teatro alla Scala, on 28 March 1896.

The principals at the première were Giuseppe Borgatti (Chénier), then at the start of his career, Evelina Carrera (Maddalena) and Mario Sammarco (Gérard); the conductor was Rodolfo Ferrari.

Andrea Chénier *a poet*	tenor
Carlo Gérard *a servant, later a sans-culotte*	baritone
Maddalena de Coigny	soprano
Bersi *her maid, a mulatto*	mezzo-soprano
Madelon *an old woman*	mezzo-soprano
La Contessa de Coigny	mezzo-soprano
Roucher *a friend of Chénier*	bass/baritone
Pietro Fléville *a novelist*	bass/baritone
Fouquier Tinville *the Public Prosecutor*	bass/baritone
Mathieu *a sans-culotte*	baritone
An Incroyable	tenor
The Abbé *a poet*	tenor
Schmidt *a gaoler at St Lazare*	bass
Master of the Household	bass

Ladies, gentlemen, abbés, footmen, musicians, servants, pages, valets, shepherdesses, beggars, sans-culottes, the National Guard, soldiers of the Republic, gendarmes, shopkeepers

Setting In and around Paris 1789–93

Luigi Illica's libretto, inspired by the life of the French poet André Chénier (1762–94), was ceded to Giordano in 1894 by Alberto Franchetti, for whom it was written. The opera was completed in mid-November the following year. After some hesitation it was accepted for performance at La Scala on the strong recommendation of Pietro Mascagni, and it proved the only success of a disastrous season given at that theatre under the management of the publisher Sonzogno, who excluded from the programme all works belonging to his rival, Ricordi. *Andrea Chénier* at once raised the composer to the front rank of the 'giovane scuola', along with Mascagni, Puccini and Leoncavallo. Today it remains the most widely performed of Giordano's operas, mainly as an effective vehicle for a star tenor. Borgatti owed to it the start of a notable Italian career. Outstanding exponents in recent times have included Franco Corelli and Placido Domingo.

*

ACT 1   *A salon in the Château Coigny*   Preparations are in hand for a party, viewed with disgust by Gérard. He inveighs against the idleness and cruelty of the aristocracy in whose service his aged father has slaved all his life as a gardener. The Countess enters and gives orders to the servants. With her are Maddalena and her maid, Bersi, who discuss clothes. Gérard, in spite of himself, nurses a hopeless passion for Maddalena. The guests begin to arrive; Fléville, the novelist, presents two friends, the Italian pianist Florinelli and the poet Andrea Chénier. They are joined by the Abbé, who brings the latest news from Paris. The King has taken the advice of Necker and summoned the Third Estate; the statue of Henri IV has been defaced by an unruly mob. To cheer the dejected company Fléville calls on the musicians to perform a madrigal to his own words, 'O pastorelle, addio'. Maddalena and her friends determine to tease Chénier out of his silence. Will he not recite a poem for them? He replies that poetry, like love, cannot be compelled; nonetheless he obliges with the Improvviso, 'Un dì all'azzurro spazio'. His love, he says, is the fair land of France, whose peasants are suffering while its clergy grows fat. The guests are offended; but the Countess begs their indulgence for a poet's wayward fancy. She commands a gavotte. But hardly has it begun when a lugubrious chant is heard from outside. Gérard comes in leading a crowd of beggars. Furious, the Countess orders them out of the house. Gérard's father goes on his knees to her; but his son raises him up, strips off his own livery and leads him and the beggars away. Recovering from a faint, the Countess declares herself totally bewildered – had she not always been generous to the poor? She bids the dance resume.

ACT 2   *The Café Hottot, by the Pont de Peronnet*   Three years have passed. Mathieu is present with a number of *sans-culottes* (republicans); Chénier sits at a table apart. Paper-boys announce the arrest of the King. Bersi arrives, followed by an Incroyable (dandy) whom she suspects of spying on her as an enemy of the Revolution. Accordingly she bursts out in its praise and joins in the cheers as a cartload of condemned prisoners passes by, to the strains of 'Ah, ça ira'. However, the Incroyable has seen her looking at Chénier and decides not to let her out of his sight. Roucher comes with a passport for Chénier, whom he advises to leave France with all speed. But Chénier has been intrigued by the receipt of letters written in a female hand and signed 'Hope'. A crowd gathers to watch the People's Representatives crossing the bridge. Among them the Incroyable notices Gérard, and draws him aside. From their conversation it appears that Gérard is in pursuit of Maddalena. The Incroyable promises to bring her to him that evening. Bersi now approaches Roucher; she has a message for Chénier: he must wait for 'Hope' at the nearby altar of Marat. She is overheard by the Incroyable. As Mathieu sings the *Carmagnole* a patrol passes by. Maddalena arrives, reveals her identity to Chénier and throws herself on his protection. The Incroyable goes off to summon Gérard. There follows a love duet between Maddalena and Chénier, 'Ecco l'altare', at the end of which Gérard appears. The two men fight. Gérard, severely wounded, recognizes Chénier and tells him to save himself and protect Maddalena. When the *sans-culottes* return and ask him who his assailant was, Gérard professes ignorance.

ACT 3   *The Hall of the Revolutionary Tribunal*   To an assembled audience Mathieu declares that the country is in danger, threatened by rebellion from within and invasion from foreign powers. Gérard enters, to receive congratulations on his recovery. He calls on the women to give their sons and their jewelry to the nation. Old Madelon comes forward. Her son, she says, died fighting for his country; but she gladly offers her 15-year-old grandson to take his father's place. Much moved, the crowd disperse to the strains of the *Carmagnole*. Newspaper vendors proclaim the arrest of Andrea Chénier. The Incroyable assures Gérard that this will draw Maddalena into the trap. As he makes out the papers of accusation Gérard reflects in a famous monologue, 'Nemico della patria', that, once the slave of the aristocracy, he has now become a slave to his own passions. Maddalena is brought before him. To his ardent declaration of love she replies with an account of her miserable existence since her mother died and their castle was burnt, 'La mamma morta', until the voice of love bade her take heart and hope. Nonetheless she is prepared to yield to Gérard if she can thereby save Chénier's life. Deeply moved and remorseful, Gérard decides to defend his rival. The court assembles and the accused are led in, among them Chénier. Fouquier Tinville reads aloud the charges against him. Chénier stoutly defends himself as a patriot and a man of honour ('Sì, fui soldato'). Tinville calls for witnesses, whereupon Gérard springs up and insists that all the accusations against his rival are false. The court is astonished, but resolved nonetheless on Chénier's execution.

ACT 4 *The courtyard of the St Lazare prison* Chénier sits at a table, writing. Schmidt, the gaoler, admits Roucher, to whom Chénier reads his final poem, 'Come un bel dì di maggio', in which he compares the sunset of his life to that of a fine spring day. Roucher leaves; the distant voice of Mathieu can be heard singing the *Marseillaise*. Then Gérard is introduced together with Maddalena. She bribes the gaoler to allow her to take the place of one of the condemned. When Gérard has left she and Chénier join in a heroic duet, 'Vicino a te s'acqueta', before being taken to the guillotine.

*

Like most *verismo* operas of the period *Andrea Chénier* is built, act by act, as a loosely organized continuity bound together by variegated orchestral figuration in which motifs, repeated at short range and in different keys, play a prominent part. Thematic recollection, however, is rare, being confined here to the final strain of Maddalena's 'La mamma morta'. The vocal delivery is naturalistic, freely mixing conversational, lyrical and declamatory elements. Solos and duets arise directly and without preparation from the dialogue and are rarely marked off by a full close. The aristocratic ambience of Act 1 is conveyed by touches of period stylization such as the gavotte, while snatches of the *Carmagnole*, 'Ah, ça ira', and the *Marseillaise* evoke the atmosphere of the Revolution.

J.B.

Fedora

Opera in three acts set to a libretto by Arturo Colautti after Victorien Sardou's play; first performed in Milan, at the Teatro Lirico, on 17 November 1898.

The much acclaimed première was conducted by the composer, with Gemma Bellincioni as Fedora, Enrico Caruso as Loris and Delfino Menotti as De Siriex.

*

Princess Fedora Romazov (soprano) is about to be married to Count Vladimir Andreyevich, captain of the Imperial Guard. Her love for him is symbolized in the Massenet-like theme of the prelude, which forms the first of the opera's two main recurring motifs. However, in the opening scene, at Andreyevich's house in St Petersburg, the servants leave no doubt that he is marrying the princess in order to restore his ruined fortunes. Fedora enters, expecting to meet him ('O grandi gli occhi lucenti'), but when he arrives home it is on a stretcher, fatally wounded. The police chief Grech (bass) interrogates the witnesses: Cirillo (baritone), the coachman who heard two shots fired, the diplomat De Siriex (baritone), who traced bloodstains in the snow to a pavilion where the count's body was found, and the groom, Dmitry (contralto), who remembers the delivery of a letter which was later removed by a visitor. His name was Count Loris Ipanov, who, it turns out, has fled the country. Fedora swears to bring him to justice as Vladimir's murderer.

Act 2 is set in Paris at the house of Fedora, who has succeeded in tracking down her enemy. She has invited him to a party in her house, intending to unmask him. Among her guests are De Siriex and the Countess Olga Sukarov (soprano) who has brought with her a Polish pianist, who claims to be Chopin's nephew. De Siriex teases Olga with a song about Russian women, 'La donna russa è femmina due volte'; she retorts with another about the Parisian male, 'Il parigino è come il vino'. Loris (tenor) enters with Fedora. His friend Borov (baritone) warns him to beware of his hostess; but Loris declares that he is already in love with her. During their flirtation he maintains that she clearly returns his feelings; his aria, 'Amor ti vieta', will furnish the second of the opera's two important motifs. While the Polish pianist plays one of his own nocturnes, Fedora draws from Loris the admission that he has left Russia as a fugitive from justice, having killed a man. He promises to tell her the whole story after the guests have left. De Siriex reads out a telegram reporting an attempt on the tsar's life, whereupon the party disperses. Fedora meanwhile reports Loris's confession to Grech, who accordingly stations his men in the garden with orders to seize the count the moment he leaves the house. Loris reappears. In a long narrative, 'Mia madre, la mia vecchia madre', he tells Fedora how he married a poor young girl, now dead, much against his mother's wishes and installed her in a pavilion in St Petersburg, and how he discovered that she was being visited by a lover, one of whose letters he intercepted. The writer was Vladimir Andreyevich. In it he mentioned his forthcoming marriage to Fedora, adding that it would make no difference to their relationship. To prove it, Loris produces the letter, to the astonishment and humiliation of Fedora, who now insists that Loris remain with her that night. The scene concludes with a love duet, 'Lascia che pianga io solo', the opening of which is recalled in the act that follows.

In Act 3 Loris and Fedora are living happily together in the Bernese Oberland. With them is Olga, who has taken up bicycling. De Siriex arrives with disturbing news. Fedora's report to Grech has reached the ears of the murdered man's father, who has had Loris's brother arrested as an accomplice and then drowned. The shock has caused their mother to die of grief. When De Siriex and Olga have left, Fedora prays that all this may be kept from Loris ('Dio di giustizia'). A postman comes with a letter from Borov recounting the sad events. Fedora confesses her responsibility and begs Loris to forgive her. When he curses her roundly she takes poison and dies in the arms of her remorseful lover.

*

Ever since seeing a performance of Sardou's play in Naples in 1885, with Sarah Bernhardt in the title role, Giordano had wanted to make an opera of it. Sardou withheld his permission until after the success of *Andrea Chénier*. *Fedora* has proved Giordano's second most popular opera, after *Andrea Chénier*. Famous interpreters of the name part have included Lina Cavalieri, Gilda dalla Rizza, Maria Caniglia and Magda Olivero; notable Loris Ipanovs were Fernando De Lucia, Aureliano Pertile, Beniamino Gigli and Giacinto Prandelli. For a film version made in 1942, Giordano provided some extra music.

In *Fedora* Giordano made abundant use of national idioms. The opening chorus of Act 1 features Russian irregular rhythms; the melody of De Siriex's solo in Act 2 is adapted from a song by the Russian composer Alexander Alyab'yev; and the dance that precedes the exeunt of the guests recalls Glinka's 'Kamarinskaya'. The Polish pianist is introduced by a polonaise, and his own nocturne parodies the style of Chopin. Act 3 opens with a *ranz des vaches* on the horn and later features a folksong-like ditty sung by an offstage treble to the accompaniment of a concertina. Touches of modernity include an electric bell in Act 1 and the appearance in Act 3 of the Countess Olga clad in bloomers and wheeling a bicycle.

J.B.

Ruggero Leoncavallo

Ruggero [Ruggiero] Leoncavallo was born in Naples on 23 April 1857; he died in Montecatini on 9 August 1919. The son of a well-to-do family in Naples – his father, Vincenzo, was a magistrate – he began his musical studies at the Conservatory in 1866. There he studied the piano with Beniamino Cesi and composition with Lauro Rossi, one of the best known opera composers of the day in the French tradition. He also studied composition under Serao until 1876. Formative in his development were the courses of the poet Giosuè Carducci, an enthusiastic Wagnerian, at Bologna University, which Leoncavallo followed from the autumn of 1876, breaking off, however, the following year without obtaining a degree. At the same time he was fired by the controversy over the art and aesthetic of *Wort–Ton–Drama* which led to the revival of the new version of Boito's *Mefistofele* and the Italian premières of *Rienzi* (1876) and *Der fliegende Holländer* (as *Vascello fantasma*, 1877), conducted by Mancinelli. Influenced by Wagner and grand opera, Leoncavallo wrote both the libretto and the music of his first opera, *Chatterton*, at about that time, although it was not performed until much later.

Encouraged by an uncle who was employed in the Italian Foreign Ministry, he then tried his fortune in Egypt, but on the outbreak of the Anglo-Egyptian War in 1882 he made his way to Marseilles and from there to Paris, where he lived a bohemian life, earning his living by giving music lessons and playing the piano at café-concerts. Thanks to the support of the baritone Victor Maurel, he received a commission for an opera from the publisher Giulio Ricordi. Leoncavallo had already decided to write a trilogy, to be entitled *Crepusculum*, which would be the Italian answer to Wagner's *Ring* cycle, as he claimed to have expounded to Wagner himself in 1876 when *Rienzi* received its first Italian performance in Bologna. His work on the project was erratic and he either could not or did not want to complete the task; the first opera, *I Medici*, took him a long time to write and caused serious difficulties with the publisher which continued until 1899. Meanwhile he made himself known in Paris with the performance of extracts from his symphonic poem *La nuit de mai*, after a poem by Alfred de Musset. After marrying the singer Berthe Rambaud he returned to Milan and became involved in the artistic life of the city, making a living by writing and occasional musical activity; he collaborated on the libretto for Puccini's *Manon Lescaut* (1893).

A decisive event for Leoncavallo's musical future was the success of Mascagni's *Cavalleria rusticana* in 1890. An acute analyst of market requirements, he recognized its significance and especially the potential of realism in opera as the quickest way to win popularity, but as with Mascagni, his fame was to rest on one opera into which he poured all his talent. *Pagliacci* was immediately successful with the Milanese audience at the Teatro Dal Verme in 1892 and paved the way for performances of his two earlier operas: *I Medici* was performed at the same theatre in the following year, and *Chatterton*, based on Alfred de Vigny's poem, was performed at the Teatro Argentina in Rome in 1896.

He completed his version of Murger's *Scènes de la vie de Bohème*, on which he had been working since 1892, and its first performance was carefully supervised by his new publisher Sonzogno in Venice in 1897. The long period of composition during which he sought to convey the realities of life in the Latin Quarter of Paris was preceded by fierce controversy with Puccini and the Ricordi publishing house. It was Leoncavallo who first had the idea of making it into an opera, but his *Bohème*, although it has pages full of vitality, is much more a social document of the period, and after the first years in which the two operas were performed almost side by side, it was Puccini's version that survived in the repertory. *Zazà*, on the other hand, the favourite role of Emma Carelli, first performed at the Teatro Lirico in Milan in 1900, was another opera with a theatrical setting and was an international success. But Leoncavallo's fortunes in Italy gradually declined, not least because being litigious by nature he frequently quarrelled with his publishers.

Although it became difficult for Leoncavallo to have his works performed in Italy they were very successful in Germany, where

PLATE 1

Giacomo Puccini (right), with (left to right) Giulio Gatti-Casazza, David Belasco and Arturo Toscanini in New York aat the time of the première of *La fanciulla del West* in December 1910

PLATE 2

ATTO TERZO

Page from the disposizione scenica (production book) for the original production of Puccini's *Manon Lescaut* at the Teatro Regio, Turin, 1 February 1893: the setting for Act 3 (Le Havre, a square near the harbour) [Biblioteca Braidense (photo Giancarlo Costa)]

PLATE 3

Poster for the first production of Puccini's *Madama Butterfly* by L. Metlicovitz
[Giancarlo Costa]

PLATE 4

Suor Angelica: final scene of the original production (designed by Pietro Stroppa) at the Metropolitan opera, New York, 14 December 1918, with Geraldine Farrar as Sister Angelica [Metropolitan Opera Archives]

PLATE 5

Claudia Muzio in the title role of Puccini's *Tosca* [Stuart-Liff Collection]

PLATE 6

Enrico Caruso as Canio in Leoncavallo's *Pagliacci* [Stuart-Liff Collection]

PLATE 7

La bohème (Puccini), Act 3 (the Barrière d'Enfer), in the original production at the Teatro Regio, Turin, 1 February 1896: from *L'illustrazione italiana* (23 February 1896) [Biblioteca Braidense (photo Giancarlo Costa)]

PLATE 8

Autograph score of a page from Cavaradossi's aria, 'Recondita armonia', from
Act 1 of Puccini's *Tosca* (1900) [Ricordi Historical Archive]

audiences were favourably inclined to works of the 'giovane scuola'. After the success of *Pagliacci* (given in German as *Der Bajazzo*) and *I Medici*, Wilhelm II commissioned an opera from him to celebrate the Hohenzollern dynasty. The story chosen as subject, *Der Roland von Berlin*, had to be translated into Italian for Leoncavallo to dramatize it, and the result was then translated back into German, in which language it received great acclaim in 1904, with almost 40 performances.

This favourable episode gave him fresh confidence. His awareness of public media led him to the recording companies as early as 1904, and to compose his celebrated *Mattinata*, which Caruso recorded for the G & T Company. This was soon followed by *La jeunesse de Figaro*, his first operetta, for the American market. He returned to opera in 1910 with *Maià* at the Teatro Costanzi in Rome, based on a story by Paul de Choudens, who had written *Amica* for Mascagni (1905). This was followed by a return to the *verismo* of *Pagliacci* (as Mascagni was to do with *Il piccolo Marat* a few years later) with *Zingari* (1912, London).

The final phase of his career was concerned mainly with operettas, whose titles indicate their superficiality, from *Prestami tua moglie* to *A chi la giarrettiera?*. His last finished opera, *Goffredo Mameli* (1916), was a grand patriotic work, based on outmoded forms of expression and of little musical interest. More seriously, Leoncavallo had accepted a commission from the artistic director of the Chicago Lyric Opera, Cleofonte Campanini. The task of adapting as operas the plays of *Edipo re* (to a libretto by the experienced dramatist Giovacchino Forzano) and *Prometeo* were the most ambitious projects of his career, but his death in 1919 prevented him from completing them. He also left unfinished an opera on a Sardinian subject, *La tormenta*, which he had begun in 1914. *Edipo re* was performed in Chicago the year after his death, with Titta Ruffo in the title role. D'Annunzio described Leoncavallo's death as 'an excellent finale for that prolific composer of melodramas and operettas whose name combined two noble beasts and who died suffocated by melodic adiposity'.

M.G.

Pagliacci
('Players')

Dramma in a prologue and two acts by Ruggero Leoncavallo to his own libretto, based on a newspaper crime report; first performed in Milan, at the Teatro Dal Verme, on 21 May 1892.

The original cast included Fiorello Giraud (Canio), Victor Maurel (Tonio) and Adelina Stehle (Nedda); the conductor was the young Arturo Toscanini

Canio (in the play, Pagliaccio) *leader of the players*	tenor
Nedda (in the play, Colombina [Colombine])	
Canio's wife	soprano
Tonio (in the play, Taddeo) *a clown*	baritone
Beppe (in the play, Arlecchino [Harlequin])	tenor
Silvio *a villager*	baritone
Two Villagers	tenor, baritone

Villagers, peasants

Setting Near Montalto, in Calabria, between 1865 and 1870 on the Feast of the Assumption

The success of Mascagni's *Cavalleria rusticana* in 1890 encouraged the music publisher Edoardo Sonzogno to look for other subjects with strong emotional appeal. When Leoncavallo, an acute analyst of market requirements who recognized the potential of realism as the quickest way to win popularity, offered him the libretto of a story of love and jealousy in a company of wandering players Sozogno was convinced that it would be successful. Leoncavallo tried first to follow Mascagni's example faithfully by making it a one-act opera, but apart from the larger dimensions of the work he found it dramatically necessary to use the curtain to make clear the distinction between the 'real life' first part of the opera, and the second part in which the play is performed. The triumph of *Pagliacci* was helped by the excellent cast: the composer added the prologue to the original plan specially for Maurel (Verdi's Iago and future Falstaff). The opera was soon widely performed, and in the first two years alone it was translated into all the European languages, including Swedish and Serbo-Croat (also into Hebrew for the Tel-Aviv production in 1924); the role of Canio has been the prerogative of the great tenors from Caruso and De Lucia to the present day.

When the author Catulle Mendès read Leoncavallo's libretto he at once decided to sue him for plagiarism, claiming that Leoncavallo had made unacknowledged use of his *La femme du tabarin* (1887), and Manuel Tamayo y Baus could have made the same claim for his *Un drama nuevo* (1899). It was at this point that Leoncavallo explained in *Le Figaro* of 9 June 1899 that his point of departure had been an incident that had occurred in Montalto, a village in Calabria, and that it had been his father Vincenzo, then a magistrate at Cosenza, who had delivered judgment. In fact, though Leoncavallo was aware of both dramas (as well as others on similar themes presented in the Parisian drama theatres) and could certainly have had them in mind, it is more relevant that plots based on jealousy with violent results were fashionable in both plays and operas at the time, from *Carmen* to *Otello* and *Cavalleria*, to mention only the masterpieces. The other notable feature of the opera, the play-within-a-play, also had plenty of precedents and parallels, constituting almost a genre in themselves. But Leoncavallo's undeniable originality lies in the way he was able to combine news item and play in a tragedy of unusually disturbing violence by making 'stage' and 'life' identical. This successful combination of *dramma buffo* and 'reality' was the model for other experiments, from Strauss's elegant *Ariadne auf Naxos* to Mascagni's disastrous *Le maschere*.

*

PROLOGUE   Before the curtain rises, the hunchback actor Tonio announces that the story is about real people. The melody of Canio's famous aria, 'Ridi pagliaccio', is heard here in the prologue and returns (in the low strings) soon after, transformed into an outline of intervals and rhythm when the crowd sees the company of actors approaching and comments on the sad life of the actors for whom life is performance. But in general the weaving of themes in the prologue is aimed at preparing the audience to react emotionally to the drama through the words of the singer. Apart from Canio's melody, at the centre of the brief instrumental introduction between the exposition and reprise of a gay and lively theme, a poetic melody is associated with the furtive love of Nedda and Silvio, while Tonio's aria 'Un nido di memorie', a shrewd reference to a world of popular images, is evoked by a melancholy melody.

ACT 1 *The village square* Preparations are afoot for the performance by the troupe of traveling players who have just arrived. Expectation is keen as the four players are enthusiastically greeted. Canio, their leader, invites the villagers to attend the play that evening. If the initial appearance of the chorus (introduced by a discordant fanfare of trumpets, spoilt by too many progressions) is conventional, the character of Canio's arioso announcing 'un gran spettacolo a ventitrè ore' (scene i), is striking, particularly in the mocking trills and the textual alliteration. Someone suggests jokingly that Tonio is attracted to Canio's wife, Nedda; Canio replies grimly that he would not hesitate to knife Tonio if that were true. His cantabile is introduced by a sparkling theme in the violins, and the sudden change to gravity in his words ('Un tal gioco'), at first restrained and ironic and then in the central section an almost sarcastic melody – which reappears later, in the play – is followed by a short chromatic passage in which there is no longer any pretence ('Ma se Nedda sul serio sorprendessi') and which anticipates what happens soon afterwards. The return of the cantabile followed by the *scherzoso* theme conclude an arc-shaped form which serves the development of the drama, with the violent expression of the leading character's jealousy at the centre of its structure. Leoncavallo thus cleverly succeeds in confirming the causes of the action through the music, although it is followed by the banal Bell Chorus 'Din, don, dan' which is unwittingly reminiscent of Verdi's 'Rataplan' chorus and Chabrier's orchestral work *España*.

Nedda remains alone (scene ii). Worried by her husband's jealousy, she reflects on the freedom of the birds which she envies. Leoncavallo displays his ability for imitative orchestration in this character passage inspired by birdsong. Tonio enters; he is in love with her, and tries in vain to kiss her, but she drives him away scornfully, slashing at him with a whip. Here too there is the mingling of stage and life, with Nedda referring to the script of the play that they are to perform in the evening. Angrily Tonio goes off, filled with a desire for revenge, as Nedda's actual lover, Silvio, emerges.

In a love duet (scene ii) Silvio urges Nedda to elope with him after the performance that night. This long episode, necessary for the development of the action temporarily absorbs the tensions that have preceded it; it provides the only really lyrical interlude in the opera. Divided into three parts, all in slow tempos (*Andante amoroso*, *Andante appassionato* and *Largo assai*), and dominated by long cantabile phrases, it ends with a romantic recapitulation of the love theme on the cello accompanying the lovers' kiss.

As they are taking leave of each other Tonio comes in and overhears their plan; he rushes to fetch Canio (scene iv). The jealous husband returns (to music recalling Verdi's Otello) accompanied by Tonio, whose words are underlined by muted brass. Canio is not quick enough to catch Silvio; he insists that Nedda tell him her lover's name, but she will not. Tonio assures him that the unknown man is bound to give himself away at the play later. Prevented by Beppe from stabbing Nedda, Canio dresses in his clown's outfit as, grief-stricken, he sings the celebrated arioso 'Vesti la giubba'. The intermezzo which follows contains the most significant semantic references of the opera. The sad melody of the preceding arioso returns in altered form, and the chromatic progressions lead to the melody of the prologue 'Un nido di memorie', another reminiscence implying the unity of life and art, as is the reworking of Canio's first cantabile 'Un tal gioco' which follows.

ACT 2 *As Act 1* The curtain goes up almost exactly as it does for the first act, with the same festive music suggestive of a wind band attracting the chattering crowd to the entertainment (scene i). This time Leoncavallo uses Verdi's device of gaiety to emphasize tragedy, although this is hardly necessary as the action on the stage repeats what has just been happening among the actors. The play (scene ii) begins with Columbine/Nedda awaiting her lover Harlequin/Beppo while her husband Pagliaccio/Canio is away. The opening *minuet* and its reprise frame Harlequin's famous serenade accompanied by solo flute and oboe. Then comes the comic *scena* in which Taddeo/Tonio tries to force his attentions on Columbine. Harlequin sees him off and is making love to her (duet *a tempo di* gavotta) when Pagliaccio returns unexpectedly. Canio comes on stage to hear the same words and the same music which his wife had used to her lover in the previous act. His repeated fierce demands to know the name of his rival are also accompanied by musical reminiscence. By now Canio is no longer Pagliaccio and is indifferent to the laughter of the crowd, who grow uncomfortable as they gradually realize that the scene is no longer realistic acting. Nedda tries in vain to continue the performance, but when Canio seizes a knife she dashes among the audience – to no avail as he chases and kills her. Silvio runs to help her and he too is killed. Canio's terse comment 'La commedia è finite' (the comedy is ended), completes the combination of reality and pretence.

*

Apart from the original practical incentive of Maurel's participation, the Prologue presents a problem of interpretation. The actor who appears in front of the curtain to announce the author's intentions anticipates the subsequent break in the theatrical illusion; when Tonio (as the Prologue) gives the order for the show to begin the audience knows that a drama is already being enacted. The 'reality' poetically established by this beginning is one layer of verisimilitude; the action of the opera is another, to which the play gives yet a third dimension, and the double murder takes us back to the second. Canio's 'La commedia è finita' closes the circle opened by Tonio's 'Incominciate' (Canto's phrase was originally also assigned to Tonio, but was appropriated by Caruso when singing Canio and has since remained in the role); and the acknowledged fiction announced in the words of the prologue gives further assurance to the *verismo* of *Pagliacci*, established by the actors' claim to be real human beings with ordinary feelings. The pairing of *Pagliacci* and *Cavalleria* on the stage – in spite of the individuality of each – is dear evidence of the common purpose of the two composers, and rescues from neglect the only masterpieces produced in the circle of the 'giovane scuola'.

Pagliacci was intentionally directed at the same audience as *Cavalleria*, and the similarity between them is evident not only in the basis of the story (the jealousy and the setting in the south of Italy), but also in the structure of the work. First, there is the division into two parts separated by an intermezzo, with similar proportions between them (the first being longer and setting the scene for the drama). Then there is the initial gesture of breaking the theatrical illusion, with a Sicilian dialect being used by Mascagni (in conformance with 19th-century tradition), while a still greater separation is achieved by Leoncavallo's Prologue, in spite of its clear reference to the *commedia dell'arte*. The two works are further apart in the details of structure, however: Mascagni used traditional 'number opera' technique (although his treatment is original), while Leoncavallo treated each scene as a unity in which the numbers are cleverly used, sometimes as traditional structures (especially in character-pieces such as the Bell Chorus and Nedda's ballade in Act 1 scene ii), sometimes incorporating melodic references and leitmotifs, and sometimes combining both possibilities.

Pagliacci takes the technique of *verismo* to its limits. Leoncavallo's patient reconstruction of his subject is necessarily less immediate than Mascagni's, but he gained from his study of precedents a refinement of detail, a more significant and shrewd use of orchestration, and a more original and expressive harmony. Hanslick rightly defined Leoncavallo as a less original but better musician than Mascagni. A continuity with the late works of Verdi can be found in the transformation of a peaceful strolling player into a truculent and violent man. The difference lies in the moral perspective: Otello degrades himself by murder, but Canio recovers his dignity. Leoncavallo understood the connection between social values and the market for entertainment. While its effect is perhaps obvious and at times over-emphatic, it is a necessary and original feature of the opera, whose vitality is still applauded by audiences all over the world.

M.G.

Zazà

Commedia lirica in four acts set to Leoncavallo's own libretto, after the play by Pierre Berton and Charles Simon; first performed in Milan, at the Teatro Lirico, on 10 November 1900.

The première of *Zazà* was conducted by Arturo Toscanini, with a cast including Rosina Storchio (Zazà), Edoardo Garbin (Dufresne) and Mario Sammarco (Cascart).

Zazà later became a favourite with star sopranos such as Emma Carelli and Geraldine Farrar. In 1947 the conductor Renzo Bianchi made a reduced version of the score which subsequently became the standard version. More recently, however, *Zazà* has been successfully revived more or less in its entirety.

*

The action takes place in St Etienne and Paris during the 1890s. After a prelude based on a swirling, heavily charged 'kiss' motif, the curtain rises on the backstage of a sleazy music hall, the Alcazar de St Etienne, during an evening's performance. A stage band is intermittently heard accompanying the various turns in a diversity of styles – Hungarian, Spanish, French *café-chantant* – breaking into dissonance when a couple of clowns appear. A scherzo-like ritornello functions as background for the dialogue. The star of the show is Zazà (soprano), bitterly hated by her rival Floriana (soprano), with whom she comes to blows. Visitors to Zazà's dressing room include her partner and ex-lover Cascart (baritone), her drunken scrounger of a mother Anaide (mezzo-soprano), and the journalist Bussy (baritone), in whose friend Dufresne (tenor) Zazà is very much interested. The attraction is mutual, but Dufresne is determined to avoid an involvement ('È un riso gentil'). However, during the course of a long, apparently casual duet in waltz rhythm (culminating in the 'kiss' motif) Zazà succeeds in overcoming his resistance.

In Act 2, set in Zazà's house, Dufresne is preparing her for his forthcoming departure for America. Their dreamy duet in berceuse rhythm ('E deciso: tu parti') is punctuated by recurrences of the scherzo-like music from Act 1 as well as the 'kiss' motif. Cascart begs Zazà, in the soulful manner of Silvio (*Pagliacci*), to break off her affair with Dufresne ('Buona Zazà del mio buon tempo, ascolta'). When she refuses, Cascart drops his bombshell: he has seen Dufresne at the Variétés in Paris with a young woman. Zazà at once sets off with her maid Natalia (mezzo-soprano) to track him down.

At the beginning of Act 3, Dufresne sits alone in his Parisian house sadly musing on his imminent separation from Zazà ('Mai più, Zazà, raggiar vedrò'). In his absence Zazà arrives with Natalia, having given a false name. They are greeted by Dufresne's small daughter Totò (spoken). From the child's artless prattling (a unique instance of 'melologo' in Italian opera of the time) Zazà realizes that her lover is a happily married man. Totò plays her visitors an 'Ave Maria' by Cherubini, around which Zazà weaves descants of sad lyricism, after which she and Natalia leave.

In Act 4 Zazà returns home in deep dejection, to be confronted by Cascart ('Zazà, piccola zingara'). When Dufresne arrives Zazà confesses that she has visited his home, and claims to have told his wife about their relationship; he denounces her as a slut, but becomes duly contrite when he learns the truth. Regretfully Zazà dismisses him from her life.

*

The opera's musical style combines the impassioned idiom of the 'giovane scuola' with elements of Parisian café music, especially in the diverse styles of the stage band, heard accompanying the various acts. Both this music and the intense motif of the prelude recur in the duet between Zazà and Dufresne in Act 2. There are also moments of period pastiche, as in Zazà's embellishment of Cherubini's 'Ave Maria' and in the scene between Anaide and Cascart. The world of *Pagliacci* is rarely far away.

J.B.

La bohème
('Bohemian Life')

Commedia lirica in four acts set to Leoncavallo's own libretto after
Henry Murger's novel *Scènes de la vie de bohème*. It was first
performed in Venice, at the Teatro La Fenice, on 6 May 1897. The
revised version, renamed *Mimì Pinson*, was first performed in
Palermo, at the Teatro Massimo, on 14 April 1913.

*

On Christmas eve a group of artists – Marcello, a painter (tenor),
Rodolfo, a poet (baritone), Schaunard, a musician (baritone), and
Gustavo Colline, a philosopher (baritone) – meet in the Café Momus,
but the proprietor Gaudenzio (tenor) is uneasy about their presence.
Musetta (mezzo-soprano) and Mimì (soprano) arrive, and Musetta is
introduced by Mimì's waltz aria 'Musetta svaria sulla bocca viva';
later, Musetta answers with the waltz 'Mimì Pinson, la biondinetta'.
The friends are unable to pay their bill, and a quarrel with the café
staff ensues. Barbemuche (bass) offers to help the artists, and honour
is satisfied by a game of billiards. In Act 2, some months later,
Musetta's lover discovers the attachment she has formed to Marcello,
and she is forced to leave her house. Guests arriving for a party remain
in the courtyard, and their chorus 'Inno della bohème', along with
Marcello's cantata 'L'influenza del blue sulle arti' and Musetta's aria
'Da quel suon soavemente', bring angry reactions from neighbours.
In the ensuing fight the Viscount Paolo (baritone) leaves with
Rodolfo's girlfriend Mimì. In Act 3, set in Marcello's garret the
following autumn, Mimì returns to Rodolfo in an attempt at reconciliation; there she meets Musetta, who is about to leave Marcello.
Marcello reacts violently, especially when he realizes that Mimì is present. Rodolfo is summoned and angrily tells Mimì to leave. Marcello's
desperate aria 'Musette! O gioia della mia dimora' ends the act. In the
final act Rodolfo is writing a poem ('Scuoti o vento fra i sibili') when
Marcello and Schaunard arrive. Mimì returns to see Rodolfo for the
last time, homeless after her separation from the viscount, and dies of
tuberculosis to the sound of Christmas choruses offstage.

*

Recent evidence has shown that Leoncavallo wrote his *Bohème* in direct competition with Puccini, and that the scenario on which both operas are based was probably Leoncavallo's. Since the two works were written at the same time, a mutual influence was exercised by the assumptions each composer made about his adversary's libretto and musical style. The deletion of the 'atto del cortile' from Puccini's opera may be seen as a direct consequence of his aquaintance with Leoncavallo's libretto, whereas Leoncavallo, in the later version of his opera entitled *Mimì Pinson*, tried to adopt the inverse order of vocal roles which by that time had been accepted by Puccini's public.

After the successful première of Leoncavallo's *Bohème* both works coexisted for a decade or so, but Leoncavallo's proved less attractive to a broader public. A comparison of both works – highly interesting on dramatic as well as musical grounds – reveals a closer adherence to Murger's novel by Leoncavallo as well as a peculiar technique of literary and musical quotations which permeate his libretto and score. On the other hand, the impact of Puccini's musico-dramatic vision and the superiority of his musical invention eventually made history decide against Leoncavallo.

Despite the overwhelming predominance of Puccini's *Bohème* in the repertory of the world's opera houses, Leoncavallo's has retained a degree of importance, especially in Italy. Memorable stagings include a production in 1957 at the San Carlo, Naples, and another in 1990 at La Fenice.

J.M.

Pietro Mascagni

Pietro Mascagni was born in Livorno, on 7 December 1863; he died at Rome, on 2 August 1945. He was a conductor as well as a composer. His precocious musical talent was identified by Alfredo Soffredini, his first teacher, who encouraged him in a musical career against the wishes of Mascagni's father, a baker.

His first compositions, a four-part mass and the cantata *In filanda* (1881), from which he extracted the dramatic idyll *Pinotta* in 1883, won him financial support from Count Florestano de Larderel and enabled him to go to the Milan Conservatory, where he studied with Ponchielli and Saladino and lived a bohemian student life, sharing a room with Puccini. He was incapable of following a regular course of study for long, and he left in April 1885, finding work at once with the company of Dario Acconci, who had already staged his operetta *Il re a Napoli* that year. He toured Italy as a conductor with various companies until he arrived at Cerignola, in Apulia, for Carnival 1886, where he settled as teacher to the local philharmonic society, partly because his wife, Lina, was expecting their first child.

In 1888 he abandoned the first version of *Guglielmo Ratcliff*, on which he had been working since 1882, in order to enter the Sonzogno competition. His *Cavalleria rusticana* greatly impressed the jury, which included Giovanni Sgambati and Amintore Galli, and he was awarded the prize over 72 rivals, among them Marco Enrico Bossi and Umberto Giordano. The opera was enormously successful from its first performance at the Costanzi in Rome in 1890. From then on Mascagni spent the rest of his long career treating a wide variety of subjects, almost as a demonstration of his many-sided talents. His next opera, *L'amico Fritz* (1891), consolidated his success with the Roman audiences, revealing a lyrical vein particularly in the numbers that have become famous, such as the Cherry Duet. This fluent rustic comedy was successful particularly because the melodic vitality – the outstanding merit of *Cavalleria* – was combined with a more elegant harmonic idiom.

126

Concerned to make his music widely known, Mascagni soon acquired a high reputation as a conductor outside Italy. In 1892 he had a great personal success in Vienna and Paris and in the following year in London, where he conducted his operas in Covent Garden's Italian season. These included *I Rantzau*, a bitter story of love between cousins but with a happy ending, which had been well received in Florence in 1892 with fine performances by singers including Battistini, Darclée and De Lucia. The critics were also favourable, the opera being hailed as 'a real music drama', and the Germans particularly praised its orchestration. Meanwhile Mascagni had succeeded in finishing *Ratcliff*, and it was performed at La Scala in 1895 with moderate success. The opera was rather dated, using old-fashioned mannerisms from Verdi and melodies reminiscent of Ponchielli which jarred after the novelties of *Manon Lescaut* and *Falstaff*. To satisfy Sonzogno Mascagni also had to write *Silvano* in a great hurry for the same season, and this was savaged by audience and critics alike.

In 1895 Mascagni was also appointed director of the Liceo Musicale of Pesaro, where his one-act opera *Zanetto* (1896) was performed, but his commitments to the operatic seasons prevented him from fulfilling his academic duties adequately, and he had to resign after he went on a long tour of the USA and Canada in 1902–3. *Iris*, with its Japanese setting, which had its première in Rome (1898) and was then performed, with minor revisions, at La Scala with considerable success, inaugurated the vogue for *fin-de-siècle* exotic opera. At the height of his popularity, Mascagni produced a resounding failure in *Le maschere* (1901), which opened simultaneously at seven Italian theatres and was a fiasco at all of them except in Rome, where it was saved by the composer's presence as conductor. The fault was laid on his falling into mannerism, but it was due rather to the impossibility of a reconciliation of Illica's wish to revive the *commedia dell'arte* with the natural vitality of the composer which was unsuited to sophisticated intellectual attempts at reviving it.

He was more successful at Monte Carlo in 1905 with *Amica*, to a French libretto by the publisher Paul de Choudens, which signalled a return to *verismo* and a renewed attention to orchestral models. At the many Italian performances of it that he conducted Mascagni included Tchaikovsky's Sixth Symphony in the programme. True success, however, returned with *Isabeau* (1911), written as a South American answer to Puccini's recent début at the New York Metropolitan with *La fanciulla del West*. Enthusiastically welcomed by the Italian community in Buenos Aires, its triumph was repeated in Milan and Venice, where it received its European première. But this voluntary return to a romantic atmosphere made it evident that Mascagni's inventiveness was exhausted and that he was acquiring a mannered style which could be reinvigorated only by his constantly seeking new subjects for treatment. His momentous collaboration with D'Annunzio, a risky partner whom Puccini had carefully avoided, resulted in *Parisina*, a 'cultured' opera which the critics unhesitatingly condemned. The following year Mascagni continued to experiment by writing for the cinema – a *Rapsodia satanica* for the film of the same name by Nino Oxilia (1915).

With *Lodoletta*, by Ouida (1917), he returned to the sentimental lyrical genre in close rivalry with Puccini's *La rondine*, and with *Sì* he made another foray into the world of operetta. Their more successful workmanship confirms Mascagni's propensity towards a balance of lyricism and drama, but feeling he had won his way back into public favour he returned to *verismo* with *Il piccolo Marat* (1921). Probably realizing at this juncture that his career was leading him inexorably to regress, he shut himself up, in spite of the work's success, in almost total seclusion, interrupted only by a revival of his youthful *Pinotta* in 1932, the 'symphonic vision' *Guardando la Santa Teresa del Bernini* and finally *Nerone* (1935). Mascagni hoped that this last work, written for himself and refused by every publisher, represented a new direction dictated by genuine inspiration, believing that he had created through the metaphor of history a new relationship with reality. His fame was briefly revived, largely through the Fascist regime which was responsible for its elaborate première at La Scala in which Aureliano Pertile shone in the leading role. It was Mascagni's last battle against the modernism of his times, and the regime was probably grateful to him for it. Celebrating the 50th anniversary of *Cavalleria*, the priest and musician Licinio Refice defined him as 'the musical lymph of pure Italianity; flame of the intact Italian tradition of melodrama; a vigilant sword to protect the artistic strength of the Italian race'. He died in 1945, in a Rome now free from totalitarianism and full of the ghosts of his triumphs.

M.G.

Cavalleria rusticana
('Rustic Chivalry')

Melodramma in one act set to a libretto by Giovanni Targioni-Tozzetti and Guido Menasci after Giovanni Verga's play based on his story; first performed at Rome, at the Teatro Costanzi, on 17 May 1890.

The singers in the first performance included Gemma Bellincioni (Santuzza) and Roberto Stagno (Turridu), later husband and wife; the conductor was Leopoldo Mugnone.

Santuzza *a young peasant woman*	soprano
Turiddu *a young peasant*	tenor
Lucia *his mother, an innkeeper*	contralto
Alfio *a carrier*	baritone
Lola *Alfio's wife*	mezzo-soprano

Villagers

Setting A village in Sicily on Easter Sunday 1880

Verga's play *Cavalleria rusticana* received its first performance in the Teatro Carignano, Turin, on 14 January 1884 with Eleanora Duse as Santuzza. Mascagni saw it less than a month later in Milan but did not think of making it into an opera until June 1888, when he read in *Il secolo* that the publisher Edoardo Sonzogno had announced the second competition for a one-act opera (Puccini had unsuccessfully submitted *Le villi* for the first). Mascagni commissioned the libretto from his fellow-citizen Targioni-Tozzetti who, worried about his ability to satisfy the precise terms of the competition, enlisted the help of another Livornese writer, Menasci. The libretto was ready in December 1888, the opera in May 1889; part of it was sent to Puccini and he in turn sent it to the publisher Giulio Ricordi, who failed to realize its worth, thus losing a golden opportunity. Needless to say, the opera won the competition and made a fortune for Sonzogno, who had arranged that the short season of the Teatro Costanzi in

Rome would include the operas of the three finalists. Mascagni's masterpiece was a resounding success and within a few months had been rapturously received in all the principal cities of Europe and America. For over a century it has found a place in the repertory of leading singers and conductors from Mahler, who conducted it in Budapest and included it in the programmes of the Vienna Staatsoper, through Hermann Levi and Felix Weingartner and on to Herbert von Karajan, among more recent performers. Today *Cavalleria* is usually paired with Leoncavallo's *Pagliacci*, a work of similar concision from which it has become virtually inseparable.

*

During the prelude Mascagni's instinct was primarily to create, through a series of continuous scenes, a fluid background to the individual passions. In the first scene, devoted to the Sicilian peasants, the atmosphere of an important religious feast is conveyed by an attractive orchestral waltz, a barrel-organ piece above which the chorus is heard and which reappears when the church service is over. Turiddu's entrance is delayed until interest in him has been aroused by the siciliana. In a dramatic dialogue Santuzza starts to tell Mamma Lucia about the sorry situation but they are interrupted by the arrival of Alfio. He asks for Turridu, and is told that he is away fetching wine supplies for the tavern; but Alfio says that he saw Turridu only that morning near his house. Alfio makes his entrance with a character-piece ('Il cavallo scalpita') in which, like Bizet's toreador, he boasts about his occupation, accompanied by the chorus; but there is in his song an element of ambiguity arising from the syncopation and the sinister nature of the melody and harmony in the middle section, which give the lie without a trace of irony to Alfio's words ('Mi aspetta a casa Lola, che m'ama e mi consola').

As he leaves, Santuzza leads the chorus of peasants in the Easter hymn, the powerful prayer ('Inneggiamo, il Signor non è morto') that follows the *Regina coeli* of the offstage chorus. The tripartite Romanza e Scena rounds out her portrait in a generous and sensuous but elegant vocal line that remains within the traditional stylized limits: the middle section is skilfully crafted from variants of the tragedy motif, and the number ends with a final reference to the prelude.

Santuzza now tells Lucia everything: Turridu has abandoned her and visits Lola secretly in Alfio's frequent absences. Santuzza feels she cannot enter the church because of her sin. On Turiddu's entrance she berates him for lying: the beginning of his duet with Santuzza ('Tu qui, Santuzza?'), the first of four sections, takes the form of a recitative interspersed with brief arioso passages. The tension approaches a climax but is frozen for a few moments by the simple stornello, 'Fior di gaggiolo', which Lola begins to sing offstage; It is clear that Lola is a heartless, shallow flirt; she upsets Santuzza and the tension explodes with renewed force in the continuation of the duet after Lola has gone into the church and her melody is recalled on the flute.

Turridu makes to follow her but Santuzza tries to hold him back; he scorns her and goes after Lola. Alfio returns looking for his wife, and in her anger and distress Santuzza blurts out what is going on. Alfio gives vent to his rage. The situation is resolved in the melodic impulse of the vocal line, with high *appassionato* phrases in the first violins doubled at various octaves by the orchestra, and in the contrast between sonorities and dynamics: the marking *quasi parlato* is placed only on 'Mala Pasqua', though it is often disregarded by the singer. The duet that follows concludes with a fiery cabaletta in F minor for Alfio and Santuzza ('Ad essi non perdono').

All the tension that has accumulated up to this point is channelled into the Intermezzo, a hymn in F based on the melody of the *Regina coeli* with which the service began, metrically varied and doubled by the violins with a simple chorale-like harmonization. Played with the curtain up, it marks the end of the Easter ceremony, but the story continues to unfold, the serenity of village life being contrasted with the passions devouring the main characters.

Everyone emerges from the church, Turriddu and Lola together. He invites his friends to go to his mother's inn. Alfio joins them but refuses to drink. After the orchestral reprise of the waltz heard at the beginning, mingling with the sound of bells and followed by the chorus, the tonality is raised to G for Turiddu's brindisi, 'Viva il vino spumeggiante', one of the most brilliant drinking-songs in all opera. It conveys well the atmosphere of nervous excitement surrounding

Turiddu and Alfio at the moment of the challenge and prepares the tragic ending. As the women nervously withdraw, Alfio challenges his rival. Turridu bids farewell to his mother, asking her to take care of Santuzza; he goes off and the fight takes place offstage. The anxious whispering of divided violins accompanies the fragmented recitative in which Turiddu addresses his mother before taking his leave of her ('Mamma, quel vino è generoso') in an impassioned progression towards the top note, a last *cri de coeur* before the cries of the women offstage announce that he has been killed and the tragedy motif bring the opera to an end.

*

All the tragic elements of the story are concentrated in a musical framework calculated to convey maximum immediacy. In this Mascagni followed a line of logical adherence to the traditional plan of 19th-century opera, returning to the closed numbers already abandoned by Verdi: although the prelude appears at first to be typical in its exposition of the principal melodies of the work, the way in which they are later recalled re-evokes its entire structure in the listener's memory, with the orchestral crescendo of the prelude interrupted by the siciliana and resumed more strongly when the voice behind the curtain ceases. In the continuation of the duet between Santuzza and Turiddu, the central point of the drama, the reprise of the prelude is in the orchestra only, intensifying the emotion of the concluding *appassionato* section.

Mascagni attained his aim of creating an opera realistically dominated by sentiment by using formal means more effective in their subtlety than openly veristic and impassioned ones, of which there are indeed few. Conscious of the need to write an 'Italian' work, he made use above all of the special qualities of the closed number and its interaction with recitative. The melody on the lower strings that accompanies Santuzza's entrance is in effect a leitmotif, reminiscent of the theme that concludes the overture to *Carmen*. In using it in proximity to the song of Alfio, Turiddu's executioner, which immediately follows, Mascagni links him with Santuzza as different facets of a common destiny, the motif itself being linked not so much to Santuzza as to the deadly destiny she brings. It reappears at all the high points of the drama, from the *romanza* to the 'Mala Pasqua' she tragically hurls at Turiddu, before concluding the opera and so revealing itself as the musical symbol of the tragic ending. This sense of conclusion is reinforced by the use of the key of F at crucial moments, from the prelude (in the major) to the central series of numbers and the Intermezzo, and to the final statement, in the minor, of the 'tragedy' motif.

It has often been said that Verga's *Cavalleria* inaugurated the *verismo* period in Italian theatre. Mascagni stressed his adherence to the play as his source, insisting that it was Verga's treatment of the subject which had spurred him to set it and rejecting the idea of a close affinity between his opera and Bizet's *Carmen*. But *Cavalleria* is as closely linked to the French opera, which, as the box-office hit of the day, was widely admired and imitated, as it is to Verga's text, which was performed everywhere and so available to any composer in need of a good subject.

Carmen was in reality a decisive model for the dramatic composition of *Cavalleria*, not only because jealousy is in both cases the driving force of the action and its bloody outcome (presented more realistically on stage in the French work), but above all because Bizet had chosen a subject set not in the remote East as was then fashionable but under more familiar Mediterranean skies, clearly indicating a shift in stylistic influence. Mascagni sketched in the local background from the beginning, including an example of the dialect siciliana within the prelude before the curtain rises, so providing a true prologue to the action in his use of a formal element that breaks with tradition but is consonant with the rustic code of honour of the melodrama. Sicily is serveral times evoked in the course of the opera with a descriptive capacity arguably even greater than Bizet's prelude and the *chanson bohémienne*.

The entire structure of *Cavalleria*, in which almost all the action occurs while the Easter Mass is taking place in the church, mirrors Act 4 of *Carmen*, where the enthusiasm of the spectators at the bullfight serves as background to the murder of the Spanish gypsy. But here too Mascagni outdoes his model, in which collective pleasure is contrasted with individual tragedy and the new lover with the old, because the church that dominates the square, and the popular devotion expressed in the Easter hymn, symbolize the violated innocence of Santuzza, the more dishonoured by Alfio's insult to Turridu.

Cavelleria Rusticana achieved a perfect balance between all its components, the dominant feature still being stylization in the 19th-century sense. Even such possible defects as the conventional orchestration and academic harmony have their place in the dramatic characterization, combined with felicitous melodic invention and an original way of handling the standard formal operatic situations so as to please both the traditional Italian opera-going public and that of foreign theatres in a nostalgic frame of mind. Mascagni's masterpiece hastened the end of an epoch by exhausting its possibilities, leaving to Puccini the task of representing Italy in the context of international opera and the fin-de-siècle crisis. It was soon evident that this national path led nowhere, and the spirit of his unrepeatable masterpiece haunted its composer for the rest of his life.

M.G.

Literary Figures

Giuseppe Adami

Guiseppe Adami was born in Verona on 4 November 1878; he died in Milan on 12 October 1946. He was a playwright, librettist and journalist. After graduating in law at the University of Padua he devoted himself to literature, first as theatre critic of the *Arena* (Verona), then as playwright.

His first stage work was the one-act comedy *I fioi di Goldoni* in Venetian dialect; thereafter he proved remarkably successful in a comic-sentimental vein with such plays as *Una capanna e il tuo cuore* (1913), *Capelli bianchi* (1915), *Felicità Colombo* (1935) and its sequel *Nonna Felicità* (1936). In 1911 he made the acquaintance of Giulio Ricordi, head of the publishing firm, of whom he left a valuable memoir in his *Giulio Ricordi e i suoi musicisti* (Milan, 1933, revised 1945 as *Giulio Ricordi, amico dei musicisti*). It was Ricordi who first put him in touch with Puccini, who briefly considered setting his Spanish-derived libretto *Anima allegra* written with Luigi Motta; it was eventually set by Franco Vittadini, for whom Adami wrote a number of ballet scenarios. His first collaboration with Puccini was on *La rondine* (1917), which he adapted as a full-length verse libretto from a German operetta text by A. M. Willner and Heinz Reichert. There followed *Il tabarro* (1918) and *Turandot* (1926), the last being written in partnership with Renato Simoni. To Adami we owe the first collection of Puccini's letters to be published, *Giacomo Puccini: epistolario* (Milan, 1928; English translation, 1931, 1974), as well as one of the earliest biographies of the composer (Milan, 1935), based on personal recollections. From 1931 to 1934 he was music critic for *La sera* (Milan) and of the review *La comoedia*. To the end of his life he maintained a connection with the house of Ricordi, for whom he acted as publicist.

J.B.

David Belasco

David Belasco was born in San Francisco on 25 July 1853; he died in New York on 15 May 1931. He was a director and playwright of Portuguese Jewish origin.

Born into a theatrical family who had emigrated from England to California at the time of the Gold Rush (circa 1850), he was educated by a Catholic priest, whose dress he affected all his life. At the age of 12 he had written his first play, *Jim Black, or The Regulator's Revenge*. From 1871 he was stage manager at various San Francisco theatres, adapting foreign plays and frequently appearing in them himself. In 1873 he met Dion Boucicault, for whom he acted for a time as secretary. He moved to New York in 1884 and achieved his first success as the author of *May Blossom*.

Prolific in every genre from light comedy to historical melodrama, he specialized in plays with an exotic ambience, which he evoked with elaborate decor and cunningly devised lighting. *Adrea* (1904) is set on an Adriatic island in the 4th century; *Madame Butterfly* (1900) and *The Darling of the Gods* (1902, once considered his masterpiece) take place in Japan; and *The Girl I Left behind Me* (1893), *The Heart of Maryland* (1895) and *The Girl of the Golden West* (1905) are stage westerns. As a director Belasco could be called the Stanislavsky of his day, while the visual effects for which he was famous owe something to the early cinema (one of his last plays, *The Return of Peter Grimm*, 1911, was written in collaboration with Cecil B. De Mille). Indeed, in *Madame Butterfly* it was the scene of the heroine's silent vigil, during which the lighting portrays the passage of time from dusk to dawn, complete with birdsong, that first attracted Puccini to the drama. Belasco is remembered today as the writer who furnished Puccini with two operatic subjects.

J.B.

Dante Alighieri

Dante Alighieri was born in Florence, in May or June of 1265; he died in Ravenna, on 14 September 1321. He was the author of the *Commedia* (known since the 16th century as *La divina commedia*), a narrative poem that has provided material for more than 20 operas: the best-known are *Gianni Schicchi* (1918, music by Puccini, libretto by Giovacchino Forzano) and *Francesca da Rimini* (1914, music by Riccardo Zandonai, libretto by Tito Ricordi after the play by Gabriele d'Annunzio).

Inferno, the first part of the *Commedia*, with its themes of sin and damnation, held a strong attraction for artists and composers of the neo-Gothic and early Romantic period. The second and third parts, *Purgatorio* and *Paradiso*, have exercised less theatrical appeal, although Cammarano's libretto for Donizetti's *Pia de' Tolomei* ultimately derives from the *Purgatorio*. The stern figure of Virgil, who in the *Inferno* accompanies the frightened Dante through hell, and the dramatic tales related by the sinners were potentially the stuff of 19th-century opera. The famous illustrations by Gustave Doré in an edition of the *Inferno* published in 1861, many of them like stage sets, fostered a familiarity with Dante's imaginary world.

Operas inspired by Dante himself include Benjamin Godard's *Dante et Béatrice* (1890), Jean Nouguès's *Dante* (1914) and John Foulds's *The Vision of Dante* (1905–8).

B.R.

Ferdinando Fontana

Ferdinando Fontana was born in Milan on 30 January 1850; he died in Lugano on 12 May 1919. A violent radical in politics and an adherent of the artistic avant-garde movement known as the 'scapigliatura', he first made his name as a poet and dramatist of subversive tendencies. Through the agency of Amilcare Ponchielli he was put in touch with the young Puccini, for whom he wrote the librettos of his first two operas, *Le villi* and *Edgar*. After the failure of the second, their collaboration ceased. Of Fontana's other librettos the most ambitious is *Asrael*, written for Alberto Franchetti, which with its scenes in heaven and hell shows the influence of Arrigo Boito's *Mefistofele*. One of his more curious beliefs was that a printed opera synopsis should form a work of art in its own right; to this we probably owe the verses which link the two acts of *Le villi* and which were intended to be read by the audience, not declaimed from the stage. Fontana was also the Italian translator of Eugen d'Albert's *Tiefland* and of three of Franz Lehár's operettas, including *Die lustige Witwe*. In 1898 he was exiled for having taken part in a political uprising, and he spent the rest of his life in Switzerland.

J.B.

Giovacchino Forzano

Giovacchino Forzano was born in Borgo San Lorenzo, Florence, on 19 November 1884; he died in Rome on 18 October 1970. A playwright, librettist and director, he began his career as a baritone after studying medicine, and then turned to the study of law. Having graduated, he became the editor of several newspapers, including *La nazione* in Florence. At the auction of Ouida's effects in 1914 he was called in as literary expert and so made the acquaintance of Puccini, who was interested in acquiring the rights of her novel *The Two Little Wooden Shoes*; though successful, Puccini abandoned the subject, which Forzano later turned into an opera for Mascagni under the title *Lodoletta*. He collaborated with Puccini on *Suor Angelica* and *Gianni Schicchi*, the last two panels of *Il trittico*, having declined *Il tabarro* on the grounds that he preferred to devise his own plots. Of his plays the most successful was *Campo di maggio* (1930) which achieved a number of performances abroad. Again to Puccini he offered an operatic adaptation of his *Sly* (1920), expanded from the prologue to Shakespeare's *The Taming of the Shrew*; but the composer lost interest after seeing the play, and the libretto was eventually set by Ermanno Wolf-Ferrari. As stage director of La Scala, Forzano mounted Arrigo Boito's *Nerone* (1924) and Puccini's *Turandot* (1926). His volume of reminiscences, *Come li ho conosciuti* (Turin, 1957), provides revealing sidelights on the composers with whom he had worked.

J.B.

Giuseppe Giacosa

Giuseppe Giacosa was born in Colleretto Parella, Ivrea, on 21 October 1847; he died there on 1 September 1906. He was a play-wright as well as a librettist. After graduating in law at Turin University he joined his father's legal practice until the success of his one-act verse comedy *Una partita a scacchi* (1873) induced him to take up a literary career. He became a member of Boito's circle, specializing at first in stylized period drama. Then followed a number of prose plays in the tradition of the French Théâtre Libre, of which *Tristi amori* (1887) and *Come le foglie* (1900) still hold the stage as worthy examples of intimate bourgeois tragedy. *La comtesse de Chaillant* (1891) was written in French for Sarah Bernhardt. From 1888 to 1894 Giacosa held the chair of literature and dramatic art at the Milan Conservatory. At the time of his death he was editor of the literary periodical *La lettura*. His output also includes a number of prose sketches associated with his native region and entitled *Novelle e paesi valdostani* (1886) and an account of a visit to America in 1891.

Regarded at the turn of the century as Italy's leading playwright, Giacosa is remembered chiefly for his association with Puccini in double harness with the librettist Luigi Illica. The partnership was organized by the publisher Giulio Ricordi in 1894. After Puccini had turned down Giacosa's offer of a Russian subject, Ricordi set the two librettists to work on the text of *La bohème* (1896); it would seem to have been Giacosa's idea to base the character of the heroine on a blend of Murger's Mimì and Francine, so ensuring a total contrast between the two female leads such as eluded Ruggero Leoncavallo in his treatment of the same subject. The collaboration continued with *Tosca* (1900) and *Madama Butterfly* (1904) with equally successful results. In each case Illica's task was to plan the scenario and draft the dialogue which Giacosa would then put into polished verse. Although he found the work uncongenial and frequently protested against Puccini's ideas he always ended by giving way to them; and his calm, benign presence at their conferences (he was known affectionately as 'the Buddha') did much to smooth their difficulties. In addition to his work for Puccini Giacosa adapted *Una partita a scacchi* for a one-act opera by the Piedmontese composer Pietro Abbà-Cornaglia (1892) and sketched out the text for an oratorio, *Cain*, for Lorenzo Perosi. The plan to write a libretto for Pietro Mascagni with Illica never came to fruition.

J.B.

Carlo Gozzi

The playwright Carlo Gozzi was born in Venice, on 13 December 1720; he died there on 14 April 1806. Born of a noble family of declining fortune, he was the leading member of the Accademia dei Granelleschi, a learned society devoted to stemming innovation and foreign importations in linguistic usage. He also set himself up against the changes that Carlo Goldoni was introducing into Venetian comedy.

Goldoni broke with the age-old Venetian tradition of the *commedia dell'arte*. In his plays, stock characters disappeared, masks were no longer worn, and a bourgeois naturalism replaced stereotyped conventions. Though immensely successful, the plays attracted criticism and envy. One of his rivals was Pietro Chiari, a prolific novelist and playwright who introduced sentimental and extravagant inanities into his comedies. Gozzi despised them both and, in answer to Goldoni's claim that he drew large audiences, declared that he could do the same with any nonsensical tale 'such as grandmothers tell little children'. To prove his point Gozzi sketched a scenario for the first of his *fiabe* (dramatized fairy tales), *L'amore delle tre melarance*, which he derived from Giambattista Basile's *Pentamerone*, a book of fairy stories in Neapolitan dialect. The play was put on at the Teatro San Samuele, under the direction of Antonio Sacchi, a famous actor-manager of the period. Two of the characters were caricatures of Goldoni and Chiari.

The result was twofold: Goldoni and Chiari, from being bitter rivals, were reconciled, and Gozzi became a successful playwright overnight. During the next four years (1762–6) he wrote another nine *fiabe*, drawing mainly on *The Thousand and One Nights* for his plots. One of them, *Turandot*, was based on a legend of Persian origin, set in China. The *fiabe* met with enthusiastic response; they were twice printed in Venice during Gozzi's lifetime (1772 and 1802) and in 1777 were translated into German. The German Romantics were impressed: Goethe, Schiller, Lessing, the Schlegels and Hoffmann all admired them, and Schiller rewrote *Turandot* as a serious drama.

Some of the elements of folklore and fantasy found their way into popular musical plays performed in Vienna, even influencing the libretto of *Die Zauberflöte*.

Gozzi's gift for satire is further seen in his burlesque, mock-heroic poem *La Marfisa bizzarra*, which caricatures the women in Chiari's novels. His lively autobiography, *Memorie inutili*, of particular interest to theatre historians, was translated by John Addington Symonds, who remarked that Gozzi's *fiabe* would make excellent opera librettos; that is in fact what later occurred. In 1911, in Berlin, Max Reinhardt directed a German translation of Gozzi's play *Turandot*. Busoni wrote the incidental music, which he later (in 1917) developed into his opera of the same title. Puccini's *Turandot* was first performed in 1926. Prokofiev's *The Love for Three Oranges*, the libretto derived by the composer from Gozzi's incomplete scenario for *L'amore delle tre melarance*, was first performed in 1921. Wagner's *Die Feen* was based on yet another of Gozzi's *fiabe*, *La donna serpente*.

B.R.

Luigi Illica

Luigi Illica was born in Castell'Arquato, near Piacenza, on 9 May 1857; he died in Colombarone on 16 Decemebr 1919. At an early age he ran away to sea and found himself fighting against the Turks in 1876. Three years later he settled in Milan and became well known in literary circles. An ardent republican, he was associated with the poet Giosuè Carducci on a radical literary review. In 1882 he produced a collection of prose sketches, *Farfalle, effetti di luce*, and the following year wrote his first play, *I Narbonnier-Latour*, in collaboration with Ferdinando Fontana. His greatest success in this field was a comedy in Milanese dialect, *L'eriditàa di Felis* (1891).

Illica's activity as a librettist began in 1889 with the crudely melodramatic *Il vassallo di Szigeth* written for Smareglia. The association with Puccini began in 1892, when Leoncavallo suggested that Illica complete the much tormented libretto of *Manon Lescaut*. As much of Domenico Oliva's work remained in the final text, including the entire fourth act, Illica tactfully withheld his name from the title-page, and the libretto was published without an attribution. In Puccini's next three operas – *La bohème*, *Tosca* and *Madama Butterfly* – Illica worked in partnership with the playwright Giuseppe Giacosa, who versified the dialogue that his colleague had drafted out. When Giacosa died in 1906 Puccini turned to other librettists, though he continued to keep Illica employed on the book of a *Maria Antonietta* which he never set; his failure to do so led to a permanent breach between them.

Illica's 35 librettos run the gamut of contemporary fashions, from near-*verismo* to historical drama, from *art nouveau* symbolism to evocations of the *commedia dell'arte*, and range as far afield as an adaptation of Thomas Hardy's *Tess of the D'Urbevilles*. Though negligible as literature, they show considerable stage sense as well as invention (he was one of the earliest librettists to devise his own plots, as in *Andrea Chénier* and *Siberia*). He was especially skilful with what could be termed the 'dynamic' or 'kinetic' ensemble during which the action moves forward (e.g. the roll-call of the prostitutes in *Manon Lescaut*, the Café Momus scene in *La bohème*, the parade of the People's Representatives in *Andrea Chénier*). Above all he was instrumental in breaking down the rigid system of Italian operatic metres into lines of irregular length, which Giacosa jokingly referred to as 'illicasillabi' but which were eminently suited to the prevailing musical style.

J.B.

John Luther Long

John Luther Long was born in Hanover, Philadelphia, on 1 January 1861; he died in Clifton Springs, New York, on 31 October 1927. In 1897 his story *Madame Butterfly* appeared in the *Century Magazine*. Based partly on a true incident told him by his sister, Mrs Irwin Corell, wife of a missionary at Nagasaki, and partly on Pierre Loti's popular 'conte' *Madame Chrysanthème*, it created such a sensation that two famous American actresses, Maude Adams and Julia Marlowe, at once sought his permission to turn it into a play. This, however, was eventually granted to the playwright David Belasco, whose one-act *Madame Butterfly*, written with Long's assistance, so impressed Puccini when he saw it in London in 1900 that he determined to make a full-length operatic version. Giuseppe Giacosa even published an Italian translation of the original story in *La lettura* to coincide with the première of *Madama Butterfly* in February 1904. Long collaborated with Belasco in five further plays, the most successful of which, *The Darling of the Gods*, also has a Japanese setting. During a visit to Philadelphia in 1907 Puccini for the first time met Long himself, who suggested to him another operatic subject; but what it was remains unknown, and in any case Puccini failed to take it up.

J.B.

Pierre Loti

Pierre [Louis-Marie-Julien Viaud] Loti was born in Rochefort on 14 January 1850; he died in Hendaye on 10 June 1923. Born into a Protestant family, he joined the French navy, was posted to a variety of stations around the world and retired as 'capitaine de vaisseau' in 1906, returning later for war service. He was elected to the Académie Française in 1891. Although *Mon frère Yves* (1883) is set in Brittany, *Pêcheur d'islande* (1886) in northern waters and *Ramuntcho* (1897) in the Basque region, most of his stories reflect experiences, or perhaps dreams of experiences, in the Levant and the Far East. Exoticism and eroticism mingle in picturesque settings until the call of duty brings things to a gently melancholic end; Delibes' *Lakmé* (1883), with a libretto based on Loti's novel *Rarahu*, is typical. André Messager's *Madame Chrysanthème* (1893), with a libretto by Georges Hartmann and André Alexandre after Loti's tale of the same name, has situations that were to be developed more powerfully in a similar setting by Puccini in *Madama Butterfly*, and in 1897 Lucien Lambert set Loti's *Le Spahi* to music (libretto by Louis Gallet and Charles-Guillaume Alexandre). Loti collaborated with Hartmann and Alexandre on the libretto of *L'île du rêve*, a three-act 'Polynesian idyll' set by Reynaldo Hahn. Stefano Donaudy's setting of *Ramuntcho* (libretto by Stefano and Alberto Donaudy) was first performed in 1921.

C.S.

Henry Murger

Henry [Henri] Murger [Mürger], was born in Paris on 27 March 1822; he died in Paris on 28 January 1861. The son of a tailor from Savoy who became a concierge in Paris, he disappointed parental hopes of his making a career in law. He preferred 'une vie de bohème', that is, a life of poverty in an attic on the left bank of the Seine, among witty friends with artistic leanings and pretty girls with loose morals but hearts of gold. The counterpart to the fun was the prospect of dying, from consumption or alcoholism, in the public hospital. All this Murger presented in a series of short stories published between 1845 and 1849 in the satirical magazine *Le corsaire*. In 1849 Théodore Barrière, a popular dramatist, proposed to Murger that they collaborate on a play based on a selection of the tales; *La vie de bohème* was a triumph. Only after this did Murger bring out *Scènes de la vie de bohème*, a reprint of the *Corsaire* material with revisions and additions. The work established Murger's reputation, but his later publications were not particularly well received.

Puccini first took an interest in Murger's stories in 1893, perhaps in part because he had discovered that Ruggero Leoncavallo was planning to base an opera on them. He invited Giuseppe Giacosa and Luigi Illica to prepare a libretto; they went back to the novel, though it appears that they also consulted the 1849 play. Leoncavallo's *La bohème*, set to his own libretto, was a success at its first performance in Venice in 1897, but Puccini's opera, though criticized at its première in Turin a year earlier, has quite eclipsed it.

C.S.

Heinz Reichert

Heinz [Heinrich Blumenreich] Reichert was born in Vienna on 27 December 1877; he died in Hollywood on 16 November 1940. In the years immediately preceding World War I he collaborated on various Viennese operetta librettos with Fritz Grünbaum (1880–1941). Then, with A. M. Willner, he was contracted to provide the operetta libretto sought by Puccini and eventually adapted by Giuseppe Adami for *La rondine* (1917). Meanwhile Willner and Reichert had enjoyed success with their adaptation of music by Schubert for *Das Dreimäderlhaus* (1916; known in English as *Lilac Time* or *Blossom Time*), and the partnership went on to provide various further librettos, notably for works for Franz Lehár and for *Walzer aus Wien* (1930; *Waltzes from Vienna* or *The Great Waltz*), which uses music by Johann Strauss father and son.

A.L.

Ricordi

Ricordi was the most important Italian publisher of opera. The firm was founded in Milan in 1808 by Giovanni Ricordi (born Milan, 1785; died Milan, 15 March 1853). It was directed from 1853 to 1888 by his son Tito (born Milan, 29 October 1811; died Milan, 7 September 1888), from 1888 to 1912 by Tito's son Giulio (born Milan, 19 December 1840; died Milan, 6 June 1912) and from 1912 to 1919 by Giulio's son Tito (born Milan, 17 May 1865; died Milan, 13 March 1933). It was managed from 1919 to 1940 jointly by Renzo Valcarenghi and Carlo Clausetti, from 1940 to 1944 by Valcarenghi and Alfredo Colombo, and from 1944 to 1952 by Colombo, Eugenio Clausetti and Camillo Ricordi. In 1952 it became a limited company, under the presidency first of Colombo, then of Guido Valcarenghi (1961–76), Carlo Origoni (for a few months during 1976), Gianni Babini (1976–88), and of Guido Rignano (from 1988).

Giovanni Ricordi, a violinist, was leader of the orchestra of a small Milanese theatre, the Fiando. Probably in 1803 he had started a *copisteria* (copying establishment) beneath the portico of the Palazzo della Ragione. From 1804 to 1807 he was under contract as official copyist and prompter to the Teatro Carcano and in 1807 to the Teatro del Lentasio. In 1807 he went to Leipzig to study the techniques of the publishers Breitkopf & Härtel; after returning to Milan, he formed a publishing partnership with Felice Festa, an engraver and music seller, on 16 January 1808. Their first and probably only joint publication was a duet from Giuseppe Farinelli's *Calliroe*, issued as the first in a series entitled *Giornale di musica vocale italiana*; the partnership was terminated on 26 June 1808.

The firm occupied several different premises (including one, from 1844, at the side of La Scala). The present premises, in via Berchet, were rebuilt after World War II and opened in 1950. The most valuable of Ricordi's rich archives survived the war and are still in the possession of the firm; housed at the production plant in via Salomone, they include some 4,000 music manuscripts (chiefly autograph), a large quantity of correspondence, and approximately 25,000 printed editions; details of much of the collection are listed at the Ufficio Ricerca Fondi Musicali (the Italian RISM centre) in Milan.

During his first decade in business Giovanni Ricordi issued an average of thirty publications a year; in his second the yearly average was about 300. This expansion was largely the result of a succession of contracts, starting from December 1814, which he won as prompter and exclusive copyist to La Scala, giving him the right to publish the music performed there; in 1825 he purchased their entire musical archives. In 1816 he had a similar contract as copyist to the Teatro Re, and in the 1830s and 1840s concluded highly favourable agreements with the opera houses of Venice and Naples. By the end of 1837 he had not only purchased the stock and plates of Ferdinando Artaria but was able to boast more then 10,000 publications, the exclusive rights to operas written for Milan and Naples, an archive of 1,800 autograph manuscripts and a branch in Florence. By his death in 1853 Giovanni had issued 25,000 publications.

Giovanni's son Tito, a good pianist, had worked in the firm since 1825. Under his management, new printing methods were introduced, branches in Naples (1860), Rome (1871), London (1875), Palermo and Paris (both 1888) were opened, and the substantial businesses of Clausetti (1864), Del Monaco and Guidi (both 1887) and finally Lucca (30 May 1888) were taken over. The acquisition of Lucca, which had been Ricordi's chief rival from the 1840s and had itself between 1847 and 1886 absorbed five firms (including Canti), brought to the Ricordi catalogue some 40,000 editions as well as the Italian rights to Wagner's operas.

Shortly before his death, Tito gave over the management of the firm to his son Giulio, a highly cultured man and the best musician in the family. He composed piano pieces and songs as well as orchestral music and stage works, culminating in a comic opera *La secchia rapita* (1910, Turin). He worked for his father for a short time from 1856 and permanently from 1863. It was he who regularly dealt with Verdi on the firm's behalf from about 1875 and who played a central role in Puccini's artistic development. Under his management, branches at Leipzig (1901) and New York (1911) were opened, part of the stock of Escudier, Ricordi's former Paris agent, was acquired

(1889), and the firms of Pigna and Schmidl (both 1902) and Carelli (1905) were taken over. His son Tito, who succeeded him, appears to have lacked both charm and judgment. He and Puccini disliked each other, and Puccini had *La rondine* published by Ricordi's rival Sonzogno. When Tito retired in 1919, the management of the firm passed out of the hands of the family. Business expansion continued, however, and in South America several publishers were taken over; the Walter Mocchi musical archives were acquired in 1929, and the Naples firm of Pasquariello absorbed in 1946. Branches were set up in São Paulo (1927), Basle (1949), Genoa (1953), Toronto (1954), Sydney (1956) and Mexico City (1958). Since then, branches or agencies have been opened in Bari, Florence, Turin and Munich, and the branch in Leipzig has closed. The New York branch was purchased by Alfredo Colombo's son, Franco (born Milan, 4 August 1911), who had been its managing director since 1949, and became known as Franco Colombo, Inc. in 1962. By 1991 Ricordi had published more than 135,500 editions.

Ricordi's first catalogue (1814) lists his first 176 publications, mainly piano arrangements of and variations on operatic tunes, pieces for guitars and the operatic numbers that formed part of his *Giornale di musica vocale italiana* (which did not run beyond its fourth volume). The most notable single items include Ricordi's first complete vocal score, Mayr's *Adelasia ed Aleramo*, issued in association with the firm of G. C. Martorelli. By 1824 the firm was offering a range of instrumental music, a large selection of Italian operatic numbers for piano solo and piano and voice (including many pieces by Rossini) and vocal scores of five complete operas. The 1825 catalogue lists about sixty operatic excerpts in full score.

By 1840 Giovanni Ricordi had, through his connections with opera houses, established both an extremely powerful position for himself in the operatic world and a highly profitable business. Rossini had effectively retired and Bellini was dead; but Ricordi had published vocal scores and was in a position to hire out performing material of 19 operas by Rossini and eight by Bellini. Donizetti was still flourishing, and Ricordi either already had published, or was about to publish, all but a handful of his works composed after 1830. Also on Ricordi's books were the best of the other Italian opera composers – Mercadante, Vaccai, Pacini and Luigi and Federico Ricci – as well as Meyerbeer, whose *Il crociato in Egitto* had been published by the firm in 1824 and whose French operas were now achieving widespread success. In 1839, by publishing Verdi's first opera, *Oberto, conte di San Bonifacio*, Ricordi took the most significant single step in the history of the firm. Except for *Attila, I masnadieri* and *Il corsaro*, published by Lucca between 1846 and 1848, Ricordi published all Verdi's remaining operas. In 1842 he founded an important and long-running house journal, the *Gazzetta musicale di Milano*, which served to focus attention on the successes of his stable of authors.

The Italian passion for operatic and vocal music coupled with the paucity of original instrumental works composed in Italy during the 19th century was reflected in Ricordi's catalogues, and during the second and third quarters of the century a large proportion of the immense quantity of instrumental music, especially for piano, put out by the firm consisted of operatic arrangements. The catalogue of 1875 advertised the *Biblioteca di musica populare*, which came to be known as the *Edizioni economiche*. Designed to be produced inexpensively, this at first consisted only of vocal and piano scores of operas, in a new smaller format (subsequently used for all Ricordi's vocal scores). This catalogue shows that in the second half of the century the firm was maintaining its operatic tradition. Carlo Pedrotti and Arrigo Boito had already been taken on, and from the 1870s operas by Amilcare Ponchielli and Alfredo Catalani were published. In 1884 Ricordi published Puccini's first opera, *Le villi*, after it had been turned down by Sonzogno; apart from *Le rondine*, the firm went on to publish all Puccini's operas. After Verdi, Puccini has been Ricordi's most valuable asset by far. Sonzogno, however, proved to be their strongest rival since Lucca; he was the main publisher of Puccini's most successful contemporaries, Pietro Mascagni and Ruggero Leoncavallo, leaving Ricordi the less profitable Franco Alfano, Alberto Franchetti, Italo Montemezzi and Ricardo Zandonai. Ricordi have continued to publish, though with far more competition and rather less energy and inspiration than in the 19th century, the works of contemporary Italian composers, including operas and other music by Ildebrando Pizzetti, Gian Francesco Malipiero, Ottorino Respighi, Ermanno Wolf-Ferrari, Lodovico Rocca, Vieri Tosatti, Renzo Rossellini, Bruno Bettinelli, Nino Rota and Flavio Testi.

In the entire history of music publishing there has been no other firm that through its own efforts, astuteness, initiative and flair has achieved a position of dominance such as Ricordi enjoyed in Italy in the 19th century, nor of power such as it has been able to maintain (on account of its rights on Verdi's and Puccini's operas) in the 20th. Yet with power should go responsibility, and Ricordi have been criticized in the past for allowing considerations of art to take second place to those of commerce. Verdi himself complained bitterly about the elder Tito's sanctioning, for financial gain, of mutilated performances of his works. There is a clear moral obligation for the publisher owning the rights and autograph manuscripts of almost every one of Verdi's and Puccini's operas to make those works available, and in correct texts. Although all the major works of Puccini are now available in full score, only about a third of Verdi's operas are offered for sale in this format (though most others are available for hire), and the fraction of Rossini's, Bellini's and Donizetti's works is far smaller still. Furthermore, there is a widely held view that the existing scores (particularly of operas from the first half of the 19th century), whether for sale or hire, often offer inaccurate or incomplete texts.

During the last twenty years, Ricordi have been making considerable efforts to remedy this situation. Scholarly access to the autograph scores is now much freer than it once was, and – more important still – the firm has become collaboratively involved in a number of critical editions, most notably those of Rossini and Verdi (both under the general editorship of Philip Gossett) and of Donizetti (under the general editorship of Gabriele Dotto and Roger Parker). Though the pace of such editions is necessarily slow, they have served gradually to enhance Ricordi's reputation among scholars and performers.

R.M. (with R.P.)

Victorien Sardou

Victorien Sardou was born in Paris, on 5 September 1831; he died there, on 8 November 1908. A dramatist and librettist, he was the son of an impoverished schoolmaster. He abandoned a medical training to devote himself to writing. His first success was *Les premières armes de Figaro* (1859), a *comédie-vaudeville* with a typically sprightly trouser role for Virginie Déjazet that owed as much to Eugène Scribe as to Pierre-Augustin Beaumarchais. Continuing in Scribe's footsteps, Sardou made his reputation with 'well-made' plays such as *Pattes de mouche* (1860) and wrote gay, satirical comedies such as *Famille Benoîton* (1865) and, in collaboration with Najac, *Divorçons* (1880). A staunch conservative in outlook, he attacked social attitudes in *Les femmes fortes* (1860), and in *Rabagas* (1872) he pilloried political leaders of the day. It was almost certainly the successful revival of some of Victor Hugo's plays that led Sardou in middle age to write historical melodramas such as *Patrie!* (1869), *La haine* (1874), *Théodora* (1884) and *La Tosca* (1887) – tense, tragic tales of human passion, usually against a background of war or popular rebellion. The spectacle was extravagant and lavish, but Sardou, a keen amateur historian, insisted on archaeological accuracy. He took pains to devise roles for such celebrities as Gabrielle Réjane and Sarah Bernhardt, and *Robespierre* (1899) and *Dante* (1903) were written for Irving to perform in London, where, despite George Bernard Shaw's fulminations, Sardou's plays were as popular as in Paris.

Sardou may fairly be regarded as Scribe's natural successor, although he achieved no real success as a librettist except in *Le roi Carotte* (1872), which he wrote for Offenbach. Most of Sardou's plays require either songs or incidental music, sometimes on a lavish scale, which was provided by numerous composers. Others were immediately attracted by the possibilities of making operas out of Sardou's melodramas, but his most significant contribution was his collaboration with Luigi Illica and Giuseppe Giacosa on the highly successful rewriting of *La Tosca* for Puccini's opera (1900). Popular and remarkably prolific in his day, his reputation waned rapidly after his death. Like Scribe he is remembered primarily for his highly emotional, lavishly theatrical contribution to opera.

C.S.

Renato Simoni

Renato Simoni was born in Verona on 5 September 1875; he died in Milan on 5 July 1952. Although Simoni's main career was in journalism, he was also a critic, playwright and librettist. In 1894 he became drama critic of the *Adige* (Verona), moving in the same capacity to *Tempo* (Milan) in 1899. In 1903 he assumed the editorship of the *Corriere della sera*, acting as its drama critic from 1913 until his death. From 1906 until 1924 he was editor of the review *La lettura* in succession to Giuseppe Giacosa – a fact which probably recommended him to Puccini as a suitable partner for Giuseppe Adami on the libretto of *Turandot* (1926). In the meantime he had written five comedies, one of them in Venetian dialect, and furnished Umberto Giordano with the text of *Madame Sans-Gêne* (1915). His only other libretto of note was *Il Dibuk* (1934), written for Lodovico Rocca. He translated a number of operettas, including Ivan Carylls *The Duchess of Danzig* (on the same subject as *Madame Sans-Gêne*). He was well known for many years as a writer of elegant childrens verses under the pseudonym 'Turno'.

J.B.

Sonzogno

The publishing firm of Sonzogno was founded in Milan at the end of the 18th century by G. B. Sonzogno, whose grandson Edoardo (born Milan, 21 April 1836; died Milan, 14 March 1920) began in 1874 to specialize in music. His first music publication was an arrangement for piano of *Il barbiere di Siviglia*. Among the firm's notable achievements were obtaining the Italian rights for *Carmen* in 1897 and, later, those for Ambroise Thomas' *Mignon* and *Hamlet*; the Sonzogno Competition was instituted in 1883 (also held in 1889, 1892 and 1903 – the young Pietro Mascagni won that of 1889, with his *Cavalleria rusticana*). The firm promoted the *verismo* school associated with Mascagni, Umberto Giordano, Filiasi, Ruggero Leoncavallo and Francesco Cilea, as well as some foreign composers, and operettas by Hervé, Charles Lecocq and Jacques Offenbach. Its greatest successes were *Pagliacci*, *Andrea Chénier*, *Fedora*, *L'amico Fritz* and *La Gioconda*. In 1875 Edoardo Sonzogno took over the management of the Teatro San Redegonda in Milan; the experiment was repeated with lasting success in 1894, when on 22 September he opened a theatre of his own, the Lirico Internazionale (founded on the site of the Canobbiana), with *La martire*, based on a theatre piece by Luigi Illica, with music by Spyridon Samaras. Sonzogno also published the periodical *Il teatro illustrato* (1881–92).

On Edoardo's retirement in 1909 the publishing house came under the direction of his son Riccardo (died 1915), who was succeeded by his cousin Renzo (1877–1920). Renzo had been introduced to music and publishing by his uncle and had worked with the separate firm Lorenzo Sonzogno, founded in 1910 to promote Italian and foreign operettas, and comic and serious operas, among which were Mascagni's *Parisina* and Ildebrando Pizzetti's *Fedra*. The firms amalgamated in 1915; the Società per Azioni Sonzogno remains active.

Giovanni Targioni-Tozzetti

Giovanni Targioni-Tozzetti was born in Livorno on 17 March 1863; he died there on 30 May 1934. He was a professional journalist who became a newspaper editor and filled a number of public appointments. His earliest libretto seems to have been *Pinotta*, written for Pietro Mascagni in the early 1880s; the score was lost for 50 years. Then came *Cavalleria rusticana*, a work which, like all of Targioni-Tozzetti's, shows a strong sense of the theatre. In this, as in a number of his subsequent librettos, he worked with Guido Menasci (born Livorno, 1867). it was said that while Targioni-Tozzetti was responsible for the passionate, dramatic sections, Menasci supplied the more elegant, restrained ones. Targioni-Tozzetti was responsible for the first Italian translation of Jules Massenet's *Werther*, and the Italian version of Mascagni's *Amica*, the composer's only work to a French text. He is sometimes credited (for example by Alfred Loewenberg) with a share in the libretto of Mascagni's *Il piccolo Marat* but the libretto carries the name of Giovacchino Forzano alone. In 1900 Targioni-Tozzetti and Menasci published a libretto *Vistilia*, 'scene liriche per la musica di Pietro Mascagni', but nothing seems to have come of it. In it they also listed five other librettos in preparation but none of them was heard of again.

J.Bl.

Alfred Maria Willner

Alfred Maria Willner, was born in Vienna on 11 July 1859; he died there on 27 October 1929. He was a philosopher, musicologist and composer of piano pieces before turning to the writing of librettos for ballets, operas and, above all, operettas. One of his early operettas was Johann Strauss the younger's *Die Göttin der Vernunft*, a commitment the latter began to regret. Strauss was forced to complete the commission only by the threat of a lawsuit and declined to attend a performance. Later the libretto and score were legally separated, and Willner revised the libretto for Franz Lehár as *Der Graf von Luxemburg*. Meanwhile Willner enjoyed a big success with the libretto for Leo Fall's *Die Dollarprinzessin*, and he went on to write librettos for several successful Lehár operettas, particularly in collaboration with Heinz Reichert. The two also collaborated on highly successful adaptations of music by Franz Schubert (*Das Dreimäderlhaus*) and by Johann Strauss father and son (*Walzer aus Wien*). In addition, they were the contracted librettists for the operetta libretto sought by Puccini and later adapted by Giuseppe Adami for *La rondine* (1917). Willner came to be much sought after for his careful working out of an operetta libretto.

A.L.

Carlo Zangarini

Carlo Zangarini was born in Bologna on 9 December 1874; he died there on 19 July 1943. As the son of an American mother, he was indicated by Tito Ricordi as the ideal librettist for Puccini's *La fanciuall del West* (1910), on which he worked with the poet Guelfo Cicinni. In 1911 he collaborated with Enrico Golisciani on Ermanno Wolf-Ferrari's *I gioielli della Madonna* and with Maurice Vauclaire on Riccardo Zandonai's *Conchita*. He was also the Italian translator of Claude Debussy's *Pelléas et Mélisande*. From 1934 he held the chair of poetic and dramatic literature at the Liceo Musicale, Bologna.

J.B.

Verismo

A movement in Italian literature, and subsequently in opera, *verismo* (Italian: 'realism'; French: *vérisme*) developed in the 1870s as a result of the innovatory drive of the 'scapigliatura' and the influence of French naturalism. Its major literary representatives are the Sicilian writers Giovanni Verga (1840–1922) with the collection of stories *Vita dei campi* (1880) and the novels *I Malavoglia* (1881) and *Mastro-don Gesualdo* (1889), Luigi Capuana (1839–1915), theorist and critic of the movement, and Federico De Roberto (1861–1927) with the novel *I Viceré* (1894).

Although sharing certain characteristics with naturalism – an impersonal style of narration, a deep interest in the lower social strata, a true-to-life approach in dealing with contemporary reality – *verismo* developed distinctive traits that marked it out as an original trend in the literature of a newly unified country. In particular, the *veristi* gave a markedly regional character to their works; they reassessed the link between art and science, established by Emile Zola as a fundamental aesthetic premise, so as to allow greater freedom to the imagination; and they arrived at an objectivity that implied total consistency of form and content. In fact, stylistic verisimilitude became a crucial problem for the *veristi*, which no one solved more successfully than Verga. In his quest for impersonality, he evolved a language capable of conveying the idioms, metaphors and turns of phrase peculiar to the actual vernacular of Sicilian fishermen and peasants. His self-effacing, highly expressive prose style remains a unique achievement in veristic literature. Considering that Italy lacked a modern narrative tradition (Manzoni's novel *I promessi sposi* remained an isolated case), *verismo* made a significant contribution to the renewal of literary prose by annexing new areas of subject matter (the life of the lower classes in the southern regions) and developing a flexible, realistic language.

Verismo also had a regenerating effect on the Italian theatre with the introduction of regional milieux, local customs and lower-class idioms. The repertory of romantic and bourgeois comedies was enriched and a new acting style evolved in order to portray the unsophisticated characters of the 'scene popolari' (as veristic plays were described). However, the emphasis on environmental elements was to turn the characteristic regionalism of *verismo* into mere picturesqueness. Veristic plays rarely matched up artistically to the prose works from which most of them were derived. Such is the case with Verga's 'scene popolari siciliane' *Cavalleria rusticana* (1884) and his 'scene drammatiche' *La lupa* (1896), both of which were dramatized versions of earlier short stories. The same is true of minor authors like the Neapolitan Salvatore Di Giacomo whose colourful 'scene popolari napoletane' *Malavita* (1889) in the local dialect was derived from a short story written in standard Italian.

Verismo entered opera through the 'scene popolari' rather than the narrative works. *Cavalleria rusticana* was the first text to be turned into an opera. In 1888 the publisher Edoardo Sonzogno advertised his second competition for a one-act opera to be written by a young Italian composer. Pietro Mascagni had no innovatory intentions in his choice of a veristic subject. Verga's play had a one-act format and already enjoyed public favour. The libretto by Giovanni Targioni-Tozzetti and Guido Menasci preserved the vividness of the dialogue and the rapid pace of the action; but, in spite of apparent structural similarities, the operatic version was distanced from the veristic play by a distortion of the social characteristics of the original story and a dilution of its down-to-earth language with traditional high-flown libretto jargon. The opera's unprecedented success, however, at the Teatro Costanzi in Rome, on 17 May 1890, led to *Cavalleria rusticana* becoming the prototype of a new genre. The term *verismo* was adopted, to designate not only the subject of the libretto but also the musico-dramatic structure of the work. The 1890s witnessed a brief flowering of operas on veristic subjects, both in Italy and abroad, as well as a large number of mediocre imitations.

Under the auspices of Edoardo Sonzogno and the first interpreters of *Cavalleria*, Gemma Bellincioni and Roberto Stagno, a 'Neapolitan' brand of operatic *verismo* was launched with Umberto Giordano's *Mala vita* (Rome, Teatro Argentina, 21 February 1892). The three acts were arranged by Nicola Daspuro from Di Giacomo's 'scene popolari'. The libretto marked an appreciable advance on the

Cavalleria prototype as regards its relationship with the prose play. Daspuro, the librettist of Mascagni's *L'amico Fritz*, treated Di Giacomo's text with scrupulous respect for layout, characterization and environment. The sordid conditions prevailing in the alleys of a big city and the *mala vita* ('wretched life') of a prostitute were transposed without softening their crude reality. The play featured the traditional Piedigrotta festival, and this was put to effective use in the opera. Di Giacomo himself contributed vernacular lines for the ritual 'new song' of the festival. Both the song and the tarantella written by Giordano have the ring of authenticity. *Mala vita* actually sounds Neapolitan; its musical idiom can be traced back to one of the most popular Neapolitan operas of the mid-19th century, Luigi Ricci's *commedia per musica*, *La festa di Piedigrotta* (1852, Naples). The unmitigated *verismo* of *Mala vita*, however, accounts for the opera's disastrous failure on its first and only performance in Naples (San Carlo, 26 April 1892). The display of the miseries of the urban proletariat raised outraged protests from the public and the local press. Away from its natural milieu, *Mala vita* enjoyed a decent but ephemeral success. In September 1892, when the opera was presented in Vienna together with *Cavalleria* and *Pagliacci*, Eduard Hanslick wrote: 'In its merciless truthfulness to life *Mala vita* is both gripping and revolting at the same time, like most of these realistic pieces.'

The second most famous veristic opera, Ruggero Leoncavallo's *Pagliacci* (Milan, Teatro Dal Verme, 21 May 1892), is a sensational and more complex work. Leoncavallo wrote both libretto and music. The explicit violence of the double murder committed by the white-faced clown is usually seen as the dramatization of an actual incident remembered from the composer's childhood. The operatic 'slice of life' so skilfully contrived by Leoncavallo is in fact the result of a subtle blending of various ingredients: a village murder, the device of the play-within-a-play with *commedia dell'arte* masks, the Pierrot pantomime as revived in Paris in the 1880s (when Leoncavallo was living there), and the open-air revels associated with a religious festival as exemplified by the Easter celebrations in *Cavalleria*.

In the following years, the customs and folkloric peculiarities of Italy's poor regions – the South, Sicily and Sardinia – were exploited by the opera industry for the production of plebeian stage works. The tendency to lapse into picturesqueness and sensationalism, inherent in the veristic theatre, became an irreversible trend. As for the music, popular songs accompanied by guitars and mandolins, tarantellas, saltarellos or other local dances, drinking songs, litanies and religious hymns, were inserted on the slightest pretext. The vocal style and the musico-dramatic structures had three main references: the scrapyard of romantic opera, the contemporary 'veristic' manner of the 'giovane scuola', and the drawing-room song style. The one-act format of the *Cavalleria* prototype was in most cases discarded in favour of two or three acts. Feeble stories with colourful vignettes were thus inflated and sustained by violent vocal outbursts, heavy orchestration, big unison climaxes, agitated duets and mellifluous intermezzos, a tendency that culminated in Ermanno Wolf-Ferrari's *I gioielli della Madonna* (1911, Berlin).

The veristic fashion spread to other countries. In France, the mature Jules Massenet composed *La Navarraise* (1894, London), a two-act opera closely modelled on *Cavalleria*, on which Bernard Shaw commented: 'He has not composed an opera: he has made up a prescription.' In Germany, Eugen d'Albert wrote *Tiefland* (1903, Prague), a two-act opera set in Catalonia. Frédéric d'Erlanger composed *Tess*, a four-act 'dramma' by Luigi Illica derived from Thomas Hardy's novel *Tess of the D'Urbervilles* (1906, Naples). Tomás Bretón's *La Dolores* (1894), Leo Janáček's *Jenůfa* (1904) and Ethel Smyth's *The Wreckers* (1906), should also be mentioned.

The constant presence of low-life subjects and the high concentration of quotations (popular songs, dances, street cries) in Italian operas following *Cavalleria* have been taken to justify the general designation 'operatic *verismo*' for this minor genre. The genre itself petered out in the early years of the 20th century, leaving *Cavalleria* and *Pagliacci* as its best contributions to the musical theatre.

The term *verismo*, however, has proved misleading and inadequate as a synonym for turn-of-the-century Italian opera, and it has been applied to such a variety of genres as to become practically meaningless. Derogatory implications were attached to its generalized use: *verismo* implied sensationalism, excess and triviality when applied to such operas as Mascagni's *Iris* (1898), Puccini's *Tosca* (1900) or Leoncavallo's *Zazà* (1900). This literary concept of realism, in choice of subject matter and stylistic treatment, interfered with the defining of the new kind of musical dramaturgy that arose after the decline of the old Romantic *melodramme*, irrespective of the veristic movement in Italian literature. Already by 1890 *verismo* in literature had given way to other trends that in turn influenced the evolution of opera, among them symbolism, exoticism and expressionism.

Verismo as a general description of the musical style of the 'giovane scuola' is characterized by a new emotional rhetoric influenced partly by Massenet and, to a lesser degree, by Wagner: passionate tension alternates with sentimental languor, delicacy with violence, especially in the vocal lines; recitatives, solo pieces and ensembles enjoy equality of status, textural cohesion being supplied by the use of orchestral motifs; and there is a total absence of bel canto coloratura. All such features need to be viewed in the context of a steady trend in late 19th-century opera towards dramatic continuity, in which the canons of musical and spoken drama draw ever closer together, so allowing the possibility of *Literaturoper* such as Mascagni's *Guglielmo Ratcliff* (1895), Italo Montemezzi's *L'amore dei tre re* (1913) and Riccardo Zandonai's *Francesca da Rimini* (1914), settings respectively of plays by Heinrich Heine (in a translation by Maffei), Sem Benelli and Gabrielle D'Annunzio; hence, too, a new rapidity of action, especially notable in Act 1 of Umberto Giordano's *Fedora* (1898) and the whole of Mascagni's *Il piccolo Marat* (1921). It was left to Puccini in his operas from *Manon Lescaut* (1893) onwards to achieve the most satisfactory synthesis and, by enriching a highly personal idiom with elements derived from his younger European contemporaries, to lead Italian opera into the 20th century.

M.S.

Glossary, Index of Role Names and Suggested Further Reading

Glossary

Act One of the main divisions of an opera, usually completing a part of the action and often having a climax of its own. The classical five-act division was adopted in early operas and common in serious French opera of the 17th and 18th centuries, but in Italian opera a three-act scheme was soon standard, later modified to two in *opera buffa*. From the late 18th century, operas were written in anything from one act to five, with three the most common; Wagner's ideal music drama was to consist of three acts.

Air French or English term for 'song' or 'aria'. In French opera of the 17th and 18th centuries it was applied both to unpretentious, brief pieces and to serious, extended monologues, comparable to arias in Italian opera.

Alto *See* Castrato and Contralto

Aria (It.) A closed, lyrical piece for solo voice, the standard vehicle for expression on the part of an operatic character. Arias appear in the earliest operas. By the early 18th century they usually follow a da capo pattern (*ABA*); by Mozart's time they took various forms, among them the slow-fast type, sometimes called rondò. this remained popular in Italian opera during most of the 19th century (the 'cantabile-cabaletta' type); even longer forms, sometimes in four sections with interruptions to reflect changes of mood, appear in the operas of Donizetti and Verdi. The aria as a detachable unit became less popular later in the century; Wagner wrote none in his mature operas, nor Verdi in *Otello* or *Falstaff* ; in Puccini, too, an aria is usually part of the dramatic texture and cannot readily be extracted. Some 20th-century composers (notably Stravinsky, in the neo-classical *Rake's Progress*) have revived the aria, but generally it has been favoured only where a formal or artificial element has been required.

Arietta (It.), **Ariette** (Fr.) A song, shorter and less elaborate than a fully developed aria or air.

Arioso (It.) 'Like an aria': a singing (as opposed to a declamatory) style of performance; a short passage in a regular tempo in the middle or at the end of a recitative; or a short aria.

Baritone A male voice of moderately low pitch, normally in the range *A–f'*. The voice became important in opera in the late 18th century, particularly in Mozart's works, although the word 'baritone' was little used at this time ('bass' served for both types of low voice). Verdi used the baritone for a great variety of roles, including secondary heroic ones.

Bass The lowest male voice, normally in the range *F–e'*. The voice is used in operas of all periods, often for gods, figures of authority (a king, a priest, a father) and for villains and sinister characters. There are several subclasses of bass: the *basso buffo* (in Italian comic opera), the *basso cantante* or French *basse-chantante* (for a more lyrical role) and the *basso profundo* (a heavy, deep, voice).

Bass-baritone A male voice combining the compass and other attributes of the bass and the baritone. It is particularly associated with Wagner, especially the roles of Wotan (the *Ring*) and Sachs (*Die Meistersinger*).

Bel canto (It.) 'Fine singing': a term loosely used to indicate both the elegant Italian vocal style of the 18th and early 19th centuries and the operas (especially those of Bellini) designed to exploit that style.

Bitonality The simultaneous use of two different keys.

Brindisi A song inviting a company to raise their glasses and drink. There are examples in Donizetti's *Lucrezia Borgia,*

Verdi's *La traviata* and *Otello* and Mascagni's *Cavelleria rusticana*.

Cabaletta (It.) Term for the concluding section, generally in a fairly rapid tempo and with mounting excitement, of an extended aria or duet, sometimes dramatically motivated by an interruption after the slower first part (the 'cantabile' or 'cavatina'). The most famous example is Violetta's 'Sempre libera degg'io' (the final section of 'Ah fors'è lui') in Act 1 of Verdi's *La traviata*.

Cantabile (It.) 'In a singing style': usually the first, slower part of a two-part aria or duet; it can also indicate an aria in slow or moderate tempo, with a broadly phased vocal line.

Cantilena Term used for a sustained or lyrical solo vocal line.

Cavatina (It.) In 18th-century opera a short aria, without da capo, often an entrance aria. Mozart used the term three times in *Le nozze di Figaro*. Later examples are Rosina's 'Una voce poco fà' in Rossini's *Il barbiere di Siviglia* and Lady Macbeth's 'Vieni t'affretta' in Verdi's *Macbeth*. Cavatinas often concluded with a Cabaletta.

Coloratura Florid figuration or ornamentation. The term is usually applied to high-pitched florid writing, exemplified by such roles as the Queen of the Night in Mozart's *Die Zauberflöte*, Violetta in Verdi's *La traviata* or Zerbinetta in Strauss's *Ariadne auf Naxos*, as well as many roles by Rossini and other early 19th-century Italian composers. The term 'coloratura soprano' signifies a singer of high pitch, lightness and agility, appropriate to such roles.

Comic opera A musico-dramatic work of a light or amusing nature. The term may be applied equally to an Italian *opera buffa*, a French *opéra comique*, a German Singspiel, a Spanish zarzuela or an English opera of light character. It is also often applied to operetta or *opéra bouffe* and even musical comedy. Most non-Italian comic operas have spoken dialogue rather than continuous music.

Comprimario, comprimaria (It.) 'With the principal': term used for a singer of secondary or minor roles in an opera.

Contralto (It.) A voice normally written for the range *g–e"*. In modern English the term denotes the lowest female voice, but the term could also denote a male Falsetto singer or a Castrato.

In opera, true contrato (as distinct from mezzo-soprano) roles are exceptional. They occurred in the 17th century for old women, almost invariably comic, but in the 18th century composers came to appreciate the deep female voice for dramatic purposes. In Handel's operas several contralto roles stand in dramatic contrast to the prima donna, for example Cornelia in *Giulio Caesare*, a mature woman and a figure of tragic dignity. Rossini's important contralto (or mezzo) roles include Cinderella in *La Cenerentola*, Rosina in *Il barbiere di Siviglia* (original version), and the heroic part of Arsaces in *Semiramide*. In later opera, contraltos were repeatedly cast as a sorceress-like figure (Verdi's Azucena and Arvidson/Ulrica, Wagner's Ortrud) or an oracle (Wagner's Erda) and sometimes as an old women.

Dramma [drama] **per musica** [dramma musicale] (It.) 'Play for music': a phrase found on the title-page of many Italian librettos, referring to a text expressly written to be set by a composer.

Duet (It.) An ensemble for two singers. It was used in opera almost from the outset, often at the end of an act or when the principal lovers were united (or parted). Later the duet became merged in the general continuity of the music (Verdi, Puccini etc) or dissolved into a musical dialogue in which the voices no longer sang simultaneously (later Wagner, R. Strauss etc). The love duet had become characterized by singing in 3rds or 6ths, acquiring a mellifluous quality of sound appropriate to shared emotion. Often the voices are used singly at first and join together later, symbolizing the development described in the text.

Falsetto (It.) The treble range produced by most adult male singers through a slightly artificial technique whereby the vocal chords vibrate in a length shorter than usual. It is rarely used in opera.

Finale (It.) The concluding, continuously composed, section of an act of an opera. The ensemble finale developed, at the beginning of the second half of the 18th century, largely through the changes wrought in comic opera by Carlo Goldoni (1707–93), who in his librettos made act finales longer, bringing in more singers and increasing the density of the plot.

Giovane scuola (It.) 'Young school': A term first applied about 1890 to the generation of Italian opera composers born just after the middle of the 19th century, comprising Alfredo Catalani, Smareglia, Leoncavallo, Puccini, Alberto Franchetti, Mascagni, Giordano and Cilea. Later it came to designate more particularly those whose style took as its starting-point the *verismo* of Mascagni's *Cavalleria rusticana* (1890) and was extended to include Alfano, Montemezzi and Zandonai. The works of the *giovane scuola* are characterized by an emotional rhetoric that owes something both to Massenet and Wagner. Although he claimed quite justifiably to have forged his idiom earlier than Mascagni, Puccini is recognized as one of their number; not, however, Wolf-Ferrari, despite his one foray into *verismo* with *I gioielli della Madonna* (1911).

Interlude Music played or sung between the main parts of a work.

Intermezzo, intermezzi (It.) Comic interludes sung between the acts or scenes of an *opera seria* in the 18th century.

Key The quality of a musical passage or composition that causes it to be sensed as gravitating towards a particular note, called the keytone or the tonic.

Leitmotif (Ger. Leitmotiv) 'Leading motif': a theme, or other musical idea, that represents or symbolizes a person, object, place, idea, state of mind, supernatural force or some other ingredient in a dramatic work. It may recur unaltered, or it may be changed in rhythm, intervallic structure, tempo, harmony, orchestration or accompaniment, to signify dramatic development, and may be combined with other leitmotifs. The concept is particularly associated with Wagner, who used it as a basis for his musical structures, but the idea was older.

Libretto (It.) 'Small book': a printed book containing the words of an opera; by extension, the text itself. In the 17th and 18th centuries, when opera houses were lit, librettos were often read during performances; when an opera was given in a language other than that of the audience, librettos were bilingual, with parallel texts on opposite pages.

Melisma A passage of florid writing in which several notes are sung in the same syllable.

Melodrama A kind of drama, or a technique used within a drama, in which the action is carried forward by the protagonist speaking in the pauses of, or during, orchestral passages, similar in style to those in operatic accompanied recitative. Its invention is usually dated to J.-J. Rousseau's *Pygmalion* (c1762). Georg Benda was its chief exponent in Germany; Mozart, influenced by him, wrote melodrama sections in his *Zaide*, Beethoven used melodrama sections in the dungeon scene of *Fidelio*; Weber used it, notably in *Der Freischütz*, Most 19th-century composers of opera have used it as a dramatic device, for example Verdi, for letter scenes in *Macbeth* and *La traviata*, and Smetana in *The Two Widows*. It has been much used by 20th-century composers, among them Puccini, Strauss, Berg, Britten and Henze.

Melodramma (It.) Term for a dramatic text written to be set to music (*see* Dramma per musica), or the resultant opera. It does not mean Melodrama. Verdi's second opera, *Un giorno di regno*, with a libretto by Felice Romani, was termed a *melodramma giocoso*; the term reappeared on *I masnadieri* and *Macbeth*, as well as *Rigoletto*, *Un ballo in maschera* and the revised *Simon Boccanegra*, but it is hard to attach any special significance to it as terms were used interchangeably.

Mezzo-soprano Term for a voice, usually female, normally written for within the range a–f♯". The distinction between the florid soprano and the weightier mezzo-soprano became common only towards the mid-18th century. The castrato Senesino, for whom Handel composed was described as having a 'penetrating, clear, even, and pleasant deep soprano voice (mezzo Soprano)'. The distinction was more keenly sensed in the 19th century, although the mezzo-soprano range was often extended as high as a b♭". Mezzo-sopranos with an extended upper range tackled the lower of two soprano roles in such operas as Bellini's *Norma* (Adagisa) and Donizetti's *Anna Bolena* (Jane Seymour). Both sopranos and mezzo-sopranos sing many of Wagner's roles.

The mezzo-soprano was often assigned a Breeches part in the era immediately after the demise of the castrato, such as Arsace's in *Semiramide*; at all periods they have taken adolescent roles such as Cherubino (*Le nozze di Figaro*) or Oktavian (*Der Rosenkavalier*). The traditional casting however is as a nurse or confidante (e.g. Brangäne in *Tristan und Isolde*, Suzuki in *Madama Butterfly*) or as the mature married woman (e.g. Herodias in Strauss's *Salome*). Saint-Saëns's Delilah is an exception to the general rule that the principal female role (particularly the beautiful maiden) is a soprano.

Modulation The movement out of one key into another as a continuous musical process. It is particularly used in opera as a device to suggest a change of mood.

Motif A short musical idea, melodic, rhythmic, or harmonic (or any combination of those).

Music drama, Musical drama The term 'Musical drama' was used by Handel for *Hercules* (1745), to distinguish it from opera and Sacred Drama. In more recent usage, the meanings attached to 'music drama' derive from the ideas formulated in Wagner's *Oper und Drama*; it is applied to his operas and to others in which the musical, verbal and scenic elements cohere to serve one dramatic end. In 1869, Verdi distinguished between opera of the old sort and the *dramma musicale* that he believed his *La forza del destino* to be. Current theatrical practice tends to qualify this unity by performing music dramas with the original music and words but freshly invented scenic elements.

Number opera Term for an opera consisting of individual sections or 'number' which can be detached from the whole, as distinct from an opera consisting of continuous music. It applies to the various forms of 18th-century opera and to some 19th-century grand operas. Under Wagner's influence the number opera became unfashionable, and neither his operas nor those of late Verdi, Puccini and the *verismo* school can be so called. Some notable works can be considered number operas, such as Berg's *Wozzeck* and Stravinsky's deliberately archaic *The Rake's Progress*.

Opéra comique (Fr.) Term for French stage works with spoken dialogue interspersed with songs and other musical numbers; it does not necessarily signify a comic opera. The genre was specially associated with the Paris theatre company known as the Opéra-Comique. Some works to which it is now applied were ar the time called 'comédie mêlée d'ariettes'. Early masters of the genre include Gréty and Philidor; the supreme *opéra comique* is by general consent Bizet's *Carmen*.

Operetta (It.) Diminutive of 'opera': a light opera with spoken dialogue, songs and dances. The form flourished during the late 19th century and early 20th. Earlier it was applied more generally to shorter, less ambitious works. It is still used on the Continent for new works akin to the Musical comedy, into which the operetta evolved in English-speaking countries.

Ostinato (It.) Term used to refer to the repetition of a musical pattern many times over; the Ground bass is a form of *ostinato* used in early opera.

Overture A piece of orchestral music designed to precede a dramatic work. By the mid-18th century the Italian type prevailed and the first movement had become longer and more elaborate; there was a tendency to drop the second and the third movements. In serious opera there was sometimes an effort to set the mood of the coming drama as in Gluck's *Alceste* and Mozart's *Idomeneo*; the famous preface to *Alceste* emphasizes the importance of this. In Mozart's *Don Giovanni*, *Così fan Tutte* and *Die Zauberflöte* the overture quotes musical ideas from the opera. Between 1790 and 1820, there was usually a slow introduction. The notion of tying the overture to the opera in mood and theme was developed in France and also appealed to the German Romantics. Beethoven made powerful use of dramatic motifs in his *Leonore* overtures while in Weber's *Der Freischütz* and *Euryanthe* overtures almost every theme reappears in the drama. Composers of French grand opera tended to expand the overture. For Bellini, Donizetti and Verdi the short prelude was an alternative, and it became normal in Italian opera after the mid-century. Wagner, in the *Ring*, preferred a 'prelude' fully integrated into the drama, as did Richard Strauss amd Puccini, whose prelude to *Tosca* consists simply of three chords (associated with a particular character). In comic operas and operettas the independent overtures lasted longer; the structure based on the themes from the drama became a medly of tunes. The 'medly' or 'potpourri' overture used by Auber, Gounod, Thomas, Offenbach and Sullivan can still be traced in musical-comedy overtures.

Pantomime A dramatic representation in dumb show; the term was also used for a form of mixed-media theatrical entertainment, primarily English, in the 18th century, related to the *commedia dell'arte* and to French ballet traditions. There was also a pantomime tradition in 18th-century Vienna. A French tradition lived on in the famous mute title-role of Auber's *La muette de Portici*; and the ballet sequence in Wagner's *Rienzi* is often referred to as a pantomime because of the relevance af the dancers. The Olympia act of Offenbach's *Les contes d'Hoffmann* also has pantomimic elements. There is a notable pantomimic scene for Beckmesser at the beginning of Act 3 of *Die Meistersinger von Nürnberg*.

Parlando, Parlante (It.) 'Speaking': a direction requiring a singer to use a manner approximating to speech.

Pezzo concertato (It.) 'Piece in concerted style': a section within a finale in Italian 19th-century opera in which several characters express divergent emotions simultaneously, as it were a 'multiple soliloquy'. It is usually in slow tempo and is sometimes called 'largo concertato'.

Preghiera (It. 'prayer') a number common in 19th-century opera in which a character prays for divine assistance in his or her plight. Moses's 'Dal tuo stellato soglio' in Rossini's *Mosè in Egito* (1818) is perhaps the best-known *preghiera* actually so titled; Desdemona's 'Ave Maria' in Verdi's *Otello* is a late example of the traditional gentle *preghiera*.

Prelude *see* Overture

Prima donna (It.) 'First lady': the principal female singer in an opera or on the roster of an opera company, almost always a soprano. The expression came into use around the mid-17th century, with the opening of public opera houses in Venice, where the ability of a leading lady to attract audiences became important. Singers who became prima donnas insisted on keeping that title; when conflicts arose, manegerial ingenuity devised such expressions as 'altra prima donna', 'prima donna assoluta' and even 'prima donna assoluta e sola'.

Some prima donnas made it a point of their status to be difficult. Adelina Patti (1843–1919), at the height of her career, stipulated that her name appear on posters in letters at least one-third larger than those used for other singers' names and that she be excused from rehearsals. The need to meet a prima donna's demands shaped many librettos and scores, particularly because her status was reflected in the number and character of the arias allotted to her.

Prologue The introductory scene to a dramatic work, in which the author explains, either directly or indirectly, the context and meaning of the work to follow. In early opera, an allegorical prologue may pay homage to the author's patron. Prologues were a usual feature in early Baroque opera; in the late 18th century and the early 19th they were rare. Wagner's *Das Rheingold* may be seen as a prologue to the *Ring* since it represents the background to the plot. There are significant prologues to Gounod's *Roméo et Juliette*, Boito's *Mefistofele* and Leoncavallo's *Pagliacci* (the last modelled on those of ancient drama and with an exposition of the theory of *verismo*). In the 20th century various kinds of literary prologue have preceded operas, as in Stravinsky's *Oedipus rex*, Prokofiev's *Love for Three Oranges* and Berg's *Lulu*.

Quartet An ensemble for four singers. Quartets appear as early as the 17th century; Cavalli's *Calisto* ends with one and A. Scarlatti wrote several. There are quartets in Handel's *Radamisto* and *Partenope*. They appear in many *opéras comiques*. In *opera buffa* of the Classical era, when ensembles are sometimes used to further the dramatic action, quartets sometimes occupy that role: examples are the Act 2 finale of Mozart's *Die Entführung aus dem Serail*, where the sequence of sections shows the consolidation of the relationships between the two

pairs of lovers, and in Act 1 of his *Don Giovanni*, where 'Non ti fidar' draws together the dramatic threads. The quartet in the last act of *Idomeneo* is however more a series of statements by the characters of their emotional positions, as is the quartetfor the 'wedding' toast in the finale of *Così fan tutte*. Another canonic quartet is 'Mir ist so wunderbar' from Beethoven's *Fidelio*. Verdi wrote a quartet in *Otello*, but his best-known example is the one from *Rigoletto*, an inspired piece of simultaneous portrayal of feeling.

Recitative A type of vocal writing which follows closely the natural rhythem and accentuation of speech, not necessarily governed by a regular tempo or organized in a specific form. It derived from the development in the late 16th century of a declamatory narrative style with harmonic support, a wide melodic range and emotionally charged treatment of words. During the 17th century, recitative came to be the vehicle for dialogue, providing a connecting link between arias; the trailing off before the cadence (representing the singers being overcome with emotion), leaving the accompaniment to provide the closure, became a convention, as did the addition of an apoggiatura at any cadence point to follow the natural inflection of Italian words.

By the late 17th century a more rapid, even delivery had developed, a trend carried further in *opera buffa* if the 18th century. Recitative was sung in a free, conversational manner. Plain or simple recitative, accompanied only by continuo, is known as *recitativo semplice* or *recitativo secco* (or simply *secco*), to distinguish it from accompanied or orchestral recitative (*recitativo accompagnato, stromentato* or *obbligato*), which in the 18th century grew increasingly important for dramatic junctures. In France, the language demanded a different style, slower-moving, more lyrical and more flexible.

Recitative with keyboard accompaniment fell out of use early in the 19th century. Recitative-like declamation, however, remained an essential means of expression.

Even late in the 19th century, when written operas with spoken dialogue were given in large houses where speech was not acceptable (like the Paris Opéra), recitatives were supplied by house composers or hacks (or the composer himself, for example Gounod with *Faust*) to replace dialogue: the most famous example is Guiraud's long-used set of recitatives for Bizet's *Carmen*. With the more continuous textures favoured in the 20th century, the concept of recitative disappeared (as it did in Wagner's mature works), to be replaced by other kinds of representation of speech. *Sprechgesang* may be seen as an Expressionist equivalent of recitative.

Ritornello (It.) A short recurring instrumental passage, particularly the tutti section of a Baroque aria.

Scapigliatura (It.: 'bohemianism') A term used to identify a period (1860–80) of renewal in Italian culture and a literary trend that opened the way to *verismo* while anticipating some features of the *fin-de-siècle* decadent movement. The terms *scapigliatura*, and *scapigliati*, meaning 'dishevelled young men' with reference to Henry Murger's *Scènes de la vie de bohème*, were used in the novel *La scapigliatura e il 6 febbraio* (Milan, 1862) by Cletto Arrighi, who first gave them wide currency.

Anti-bourgeois selfconsciousness and disorderly life-style characterized a group of artists and intellectuals in Milan in the 1860s who adopted the name *scapigliati*. The poets Emilio Praga (1839–75) and Arrigo Boito (1842–1918) were the central figures of the group, which included the musician Franco Faccio (1840–91) and the painter Tranquillo Cremona. Rather than a movement, *scapigliatura* was a free brotherhood of dissatisfied, high-minded young men with a strong commitment towards a rejuvenation of Italian culture and the promotion of a close interrelation between poetry and its 'sister arts', music and painting. The literary trend was characterized by a reaction against Manzoni and his epigones and the adoption of themes and stylistic features from French and German authors (Baudelaire, the Parnassians, Heine, Hoffmann). Defined as a 'post-Romantic avant garde', the *scapigliati* exhibited a taste for morbid and macabre subjects, an acute perception of evil and a sense of inadequacy to achieve their ideals. Linguistic and metrical experimentation was a constant feature of their poetry.

In music, *scapigliatura* is relevant for the influence it had on the language of librettos and for the critical writings in Milanese periodicals (e.g. Arrigo Boito's articles in *La perseveranza* and *Figaro*). Only three operas were produced by the *scapigliati*: Franco Faccio's *I profughi fiamminghi* (1863) to a libretto by Praga, *Amleto* (1865) by Faccio and Boito, and Boito's emblematic *Mefistofele* (1868). Boito's obsession with the pathology of evil can be detected in his libretto for Amilcare Ponchielli's *La Gioconda* (1876), where the character of Barnaba anticipates the un-Shakespearean Iago of Boito's *Otello* for Verdi.

Scena (It.), **Scène** (Fr.) Term used to mean (1) the stage (e.g. 'sulla scena', on the stage; 'derrière la scène', behind the stage), (2) the scene represented on the stage, (3) a division of an act (*see* Scene). In Italian opera it also means an episode with no formal construction but made up of diverse elements. The 'Scena e duetto' is a typical unit in opera of the Rossinian period. A *scena* of a particularly dramatic character, often (though not invariably) for a single character, may be described as a 'gran scena', e.g. 'Gran scena del sonnambulismo' in Verdi's *Macbeth*.

Scene (1) The location of an opera, or an act or part of an act of an opera; by extension, any part of an opera in one location. (2) In earlier usage, a scene was a section of an act culminating in an aria (or occasionally an ensemble); any substantial (in some operas, any at all) change in the characters on the stage was reckoned a change of scene, and the scenes were numbered accordingly.

Sextet An ensemble for six singers. Sextets are rare in the operatic repertory, except within act finales, but there are two notable Mozart examples: the recognition scene in Act 3 of *Le nozze di Figaro* and the central scene of Act 2 of *Don Giovanni*. The most celebrated operatic sextet is that at the climax of Donizetti's *Lucia di Lammermoor*.

Siciliana (It.) An aria type of the late 17th and early 18th centuries, normally in a slow 12/8 or 6/8 rhythm; it was associated particularly with pastoral scenes and melancholy emotion.

Soprano (It.) The highest female voice, normally written for within the range $c'-a''$; the word is also applied to a boy's treble voice and in the 17th and 18th centuries to a castrato of high range. The soprano voice was used for expressive roles in the earliest operas. During the Baroque period it was found to be suited to brilliant vocal display, and when a singer achieved fame it was usually because of an ability to perform elaborate music with precision as well as beauty. The heroine's role was sung by the most skilful soprano, the prima donna; to her were assigned the greatest number of arias and the most difficult and expressively wide-ranging music. The highest note usually required was a and little merit was placed on the capacity to sing higher.

The development of the different categories of the soprano voice belongs to the 19th century, strongly foreshadowed in the variety of roles and styles found in Mozart's operas (although type-casting was not at all rigid: the singer of Susanna in 1789 created Fiordiligi the next year). It was a consequence of the divergence of national operatic traditions and the rise of a consolidated repertory. Italian sopranos of the age of Rossini and Bellini developed a coloratura style and the ability to sustain a long lyrical line (the coloratura soprano and the lyric soprano); later, in Verdi's time, with larger opera houses and orchestras, the more dramatic *spinto* and *lirico spirito* appeared. In Germany the dramatic or heroic soprano was already foreshadowed in Beethoven's Leonore and Weber's Agathe; Wagner's Brünnhilde, demanding great power and brilliance, was the climax of this development. French *grand opéra* developed its own style of lyric-dramatic soprano. The operetta too produced a light, agile voice of its own.

Spinto (It.) 'Pushed': term for a lyric voice, usually soprano or tenor, that is able to sound powerful and incisive at dramatic climaxes. The full expression is 'lirico spinto'. The term is also used to describe roles that require voices of this character, for example Mimì in Puccini's *La bohème* and Alfredo in Verdi's *La traviata*.

Tenor The highest natural male voice, normally written for within the range $c-a'$. Although the tenor voice was valued in early opera – a tenor, Francesco Rasi (1574– after 1620), sang Monteverdi's Orpheus (1607) – heroic roles in middle and late Baroque opera were assigned to the castrato. Tenors took minor roles, such as the old man (sometimes with comic overtones), the lighthearted confidant, the mischievous schemer or the messenger, or even a travesty role of the old nurse. By the 1720s, important roles were occasionally given to tenors, and by the Classical era the voice was more regularly used in central roles. Such roles as Mozart's Bassilio, Ottavio, Ferrando and Titus – comic, docile lover, more virile lover, benevolent monarch – define the scope of the voice at this period.

A creation of the early 19th century was the *tenore di grazia*, a light, high voice moving smoothly into falsetto up to d'', called for by many Rossini roles. With the increasing size of opera houses, and the changes in musical style, the *tenore di forza* was called for. The tendency continued as, with Verdi's operas, the *tenore robusto* developed. For the German heroic tenor roles of the 19th century, especially Wagner's, a more weighty, durable type was needed, the Heldentenor. The lighter tenor continued to be cultivated for the more lyrical French roles. Many of the great tenors of the 20th century have been Italians, and made their names in Italian music, from Enrico Caruso (1873–1921) to Luciano Pavarotti; to these the Spaniard Plácido Domingo should be added.

Terzet, Trio An ensemble for three singers. Terzets or trios have been used throughout the history of opera. there is an example in Monteverdi's *L'incoronazione di Poppea*; Handel used the form several times, notably in *Tamerlano, Orlando*, and *Alcina*, and Gluck wrote examples in the closing scenes of his Italian reform operas. Mozart's include three (one in *Don Giovanni*, two in *La clemenza di Tito*) which are akin to arias with comments from two subsidiary characters. There are two in Weber's *Der Freischütz* and several for very high tenors in Rossini's serious operas. The form was much used by the Romantics, among them Verdi, who wrote three examples in *Un ballo in maschera*.

Through-composed Term for an aria in which the music for each stanza is different.

Tonal Term used for music in a particular key, or a pitch centre to which the music naturally gravitates. The use of tonalities, or the interplay of keys, can be an important dramatic weapon in the opera composer's armoury.

Trio *see* Terzet

Verismo (It.) 'Realism': name for the Italian version of the late 19th-century movement towards the naturalism in European literature, of which Emile Zola in France was the dominant figure. In Italy the novelist Giovanni Verga occupied a similar position; his *Cavalleria rusticana* was the basis for Mascagni's opera (1889), whose tremendous success spawned a series of similar one-act *verismo* operas in Italy and elsewhere of which only Leoncavallo's *Pagliacci* (1891) remains the repertory. These followed the general naturalistic tendencies towards introducing characters from the lower social strata, strong local colour and situations centring on the violent clash of fierce, even brutal passions, particularly hatred, lust, betrayal and murder. The term is sometimes more broadly used for Italian opera generally of the same period.

Index of role names

Index of role names

Lauretta (soprano)	*Gianni Schicchi*
Lescaut (baritone)	*Manon Lescaut*
Lisette (soprano)	*La Rondine*
Liù (soprano)	*Turandot*
Luigi (tenor)	*Il tabarro*
Magda de Civry (soprano)	*La Rondine*
Manon Lescaut (soprano)	*Manon Lescaut*
Marcello (baritone)	*La bohème*
Marco (baritone)	*Gianni Schicchi*
Michele (baritone)	*Il tabarro*
Mimi (soprano)	*La bohème*
Minnie (soprano)	*La fanciulla del West*
Monitress (mezzo-soprano)	*Suor Angelica*
Musetta (soprano)	*La bohème*
Nella (soprano)	*Gianni Schicchi*
Nick (tenor)	*La fanciulla del West*
Osmina, Sister (soprano)	*Suor Angelica*
Pang (tenor)	*Turandot*
Parpignol (tenor)	*La bohème*
Pinellino (bass)	*Gianni Schicchi*
Ping (baritone)	*Turandot*
Pinkerton, Lieutenant (tenor)	*Madama Butterfly*
Pong (tenor)	*Turandot*
Princess (alto)	*Suor Angelica*
Prunier (tenor)	*La Rondine*
Rambaldo Fernandez (baritone)	*La Rondine*
Rance, Jack (baritone)	*La fanciulla del West*
Rinuccio (tenor)	*Gianni Schicchi*
Roberto (tenor)	*Le villi*
Rodolfo (tenor)	*La bohème*
Ruggero Lastouc (tenor)	*La Rondine*
Sacristan (bass)	*Tosca*
Scarpia (baritone)	*Tosca*
Schaunard (baritone)	*La bohème*
Sciarrone (bass)	*Tosca*
Sharpless (baritone)	*Madama Butterfly*
Shepherd-Boy (alto)	*Tosca*
Sid (baritone)	*La fanciulla del West*
Simone (bass)	*Gianni Schicchi*
Sonora (baritone)	*La fanciulla del West*
Spinelloccio, Maestro (bass)	*Gianni Schicchi*
Spoletta (tenor)	*Tosca*
Suzuki (mezzo-soprano)	*Madama Butterfly*

Suggested further reading

The New Grove Dictionary of Opera, edited by Stanley Sadie (London and New York, 1992)

*

G.R. Marek: *Puccini: a Biography* (New York, 1951)

D. Del Fiorentino: *Immortal Bohemian: an Intimate Memoir of Giacomo Puccini* (London, 1952)

M. Carner: *Puccini: a Critical Biography* (London, 1958, 1974)

E. Greenfield: *Puccini: Keeper of the Seal* (London, 1958)

P.C. Hughes: *Famous Puccini Operas* (London, 1959)

M. Morini, ed.: *Pietro Mascagni* (Milan, 1964)

R. Stivender, ed. and trans.: *The Autobiography of Pietro Mascagni* (New York, 1975)

W. Ashbrook: *The Operas of Puccini* (New York, 1968; London, 1969, 1985)

J.R. Nicolaisen: *Italian Opera in Transition, 1871–1893* (Ann Arbor, 1977)

H. Greenfield: *Puccini* (London, 1980)

M. Carner: *Giacomo Puccini: Tosca* (Cambridge, 1985)

A. Groos and R. Parker: *Giacomo Puccini: La bohème* (Cambridge, 1986)

T.G. Kaufman: 'Alfredo Catalani', *Verdi and his Major Contemporaries* (New York and London, 1990), 31–44

W. Ashbrook and H. Powers: *Puccini's Turandot: the End of the Great Tradition* (Princeton, NJ, 1991)

W. Weaver and S. Puccini, eds: *The Puccini Companion* (New York and London, 1994)